T0198598

Praise for Pathways to Wholeness

What a beautifully written piece of art! It touches my soul with love and ease. Each pathway is clearly stated, with each step given in its entirety. Janet's soul gently shines through every sentence. Her unconditional love for humanity and all life permeates the reader. What a beautiful reading experience, a guide to truly finding pathways to wholeness!
—Jodie Scott, PhD, LMHC, NCC, D-CEP

The title says it all: the "Pathways to Wholeness" start with whole-body mobilization on a literal path and then increase mindful engagement with breathing. The plural "ways" reflect metaphorical steps through integration of mind, emotions, and the world we now inhabit with all senses. There can be no greater wholeness or clearer map.
—Phyllis Cullam, PhD
Annapolis Mindfulness Practice Group

Pathways to Wholeness embodies what a heart-centered life can be. Janet G. Nestor teaches an easily accessible way to discover a mindful lifestyle, emanating from her own rich background in mindfulness and various healing practices. The tools in this book are pathways to discover our own wholeness and to root ourselves in a life lived from a compassionate heart and an aware mind. This book will live on your bedside table as a gentle reminder of the goodness of our lives and of how capable we are of being present for all of it!
—Brooke Campanelli, RYT
Certified mindfulness facilitator, Mindful Schools educator, and owner of SoulPlay Yoga & Wellness Studio, Los Angeles

Pathways
to
Wholeness

Connecting to the Power of
Now through Mindful Meditation

JANET G. NESTOR

PATHWAYS TO WHOLENESS

Author Credits: Author of Nurturing Wellness through Radical Self-Care and Co-author or Revolutionize Your Health: How to Take Back Your Body's Power to Heal

iUniverse books may be ordered through booksellers or by contacting:

iUniverse
1663 Liberty Drive
Bloomington, IN 47403
www.iuniverse.com
844-349-9409

Author's photograph by Racelle Campanelli, https://www.photosbyracelle.com
Graphics by Frances Phelps, www.illuminatedheartdesign.com
Editing by Theresa Thompson, skeeko@aya.yale.edu
Interior Image Credit: unsplash.com

ISBN: 978-1-6632-4469-7 (sc)
ISBN: 978-1-6632-4468-0 (e)

Library of Congress Control Number: 2022920271

Print information available on the last page.

iUniverse rev. date: 01/24/2023

To my beautiful daughters
and grandchildren

May each of you continue to grow in a mindful
way, embracing a life filled with laughter,
harmony, love, compassion, and wisdom.

Credit: Mick Haupt

WALKING MEDITATION

Each step is the walk
One step at a time
Each step is taken now
Each breath is taken now

Time before is not here with me
Time to come has not yet arrived
I am free of past and future
Life is now

In meditation, I walk alone in togetherness
I walk in my own wholeness
I walk into understanding
I am the understanding

I walk to experience inner peace
Each step I take in peace, I have found it
One gentle, peaceful step, and then another
Creating a life path of peace, one step at a time

CONTENTS

PART 4: EXPANDING OUR VISION

PART 5: ET CETERA

Credit: Dave Hoefler

FOREWORD

A sincere thank-you to Janet Nestor for writing and now updating this wonderful book! Like all things, our life is a work in progress. *Pathways to Wholeness* speaks to the integrity of the wholeness implicit in one's biological footprint, as defined by the body, mind, and spirit.

I have had the privilege of knowing Janet for more than a decade. I know many bright people but not many bright and kind people—Janet is one of the latter. She brings wisdom to the everyday—and particularly to each moment—that is rare in its authenticity and kindness. Her credentials speak for themselves, and it's with this background and brief character overview that the stage is set for what I would like to share with you, the reader.

Having read the initial edition and benefited tremendously, what a surprise that I am writing the foreword to the updated edition!

As we survey the landscape of mindfulness, contemplation, diaphragmatic breathing and, in particular, walking meditation, Janet brings to the table authority and, especially, an understanding that is rare.

Coming home to the reality where we find ourselves is pivotal to staying grounded. This book excels in offering a practicum in doing just that. As an integrative, holistic medical physician, I have found, as Janet so practically writes about, that a bunch of information is absolutely useless without a pragmatic, doable take-home message. This book is a mindfulness resource for everyone who is interested in living a mindful, now-focused life.

We start the journey with "Part 1—Concepts to Assist Our Journeys," which lays the framework for the content to follow. "Part 2—The Original Walk" then dives straight into the nuts and bolts of walking meditation—and I love this—"Janet-Style." What is offered is a simple, elegant method that is imbued with Janet's sagacity and grounded in her being. "Part 3—Enriching the Journey" offers, initially, a touchstone on mindful breathing that is eminently doable. This is followed by a meeting of ways, "Breath Walking," which enables and opens the door to the reality of the now. By using nature as a companion, we are able to focus and—by truly feeling—touch and reach into our being to achieve emotional wholeness. "Part 4—Expanding Our Visions" is a holistic perspective in awakening and healing. Janet touches on REB (Radiant Energies Balance), which is a foundational part of her contribution. As if this were not enough, she puts the icing on the cake with chapter 10, which includes a bioenergetic self-guided meditation. "Part 5—Et Cetera" closes out this wonderful book with what Janet feels might be useful to you, the reader.

Read this book—you will not be the same!
—Alex Augoustides, MD, FAAFP, ABIHM, GCMI
author of *What Healing Means to Me*

Credit: Johnathan Borba

INTRODUCTION

Once we walk within the perfect energy flow of creation, all levels of things are possible. We are not perfect but are given an opportunity to grow within the image of perfection that is shared with us and is, in fact, a part of us. There are no limitations within this image of perfection. This includes perfect safety and the ability to give up our need to defend and protect ourselves from unknown dangers.

MY STORY

Sharing personal stories of positive change and healing are not always easy, but I believe they are important. I hope my journey inspires at least one person to create a new chapter in his or her life—one that is happier and healthier than before.

If you have a story that continues to bring you pain, the information in this book can help you heal. If you are on a personal growth journey, you will find support for your journey on these pages. Tai chi, meditation, journaling, and walking were the tools that I used to bring increasing amounts of sunshine into my life.

I have not always been a happy person. My childhood years were extraordinarily painful. My great-grandfather, mother, and second stepfather were active alcoholics. My first stepfather was verbally, psychologically, and physically abusive to my mother and me. My mother suffered from significant mental health issues because of her difficult early years. My maternal grandfather was a recovered abusive husband and alcoholic. My great-grandmother, grandmother, and mother were all anxiety-ridden and suffered a variety of crippling fears and severe panic attacks. I had panic attacks as a young adolescent; I had had great teachers.

My grandfather and grandmother were my anchors in my early years. I was lucky to have people in my life who cared enough to positively support my journey. My healing began at age seventeen when I left home for college. In my early thirties, I joined Adult Children of Alcoholics and, later, two other twelve-step programs that introduced me to spirituality. Twelve-step spirituality opened my heart and mind to a new way of approaching my religious beliefs and handling family issues.

My healing deepened when I was about thirty-five. At age fifty, I went through a major life transition, and I invited more positives into my life. I wanted to be more, to complete my healing journey, and to claim my wholeness. I wanted to grow spiritually and work daily to do something that enriched my life. I wanted to provide a service to others and feel I was contributing to the higher good.

I have always been a spiritual person, but during that transition, I began to live my journey to self. I changed my career. I began a practice of tai chi, became a reiki master teacher, took a twelve-month class in etheric healing, and participated in chi healing instruction. I found a spiritual study partner to talk and explore with and refined my spiritual and religious beliefs to fully encompass the doctrine of love. I began taking classes in energy psychology so I could help my counseling clients ease their anxiety, depression, grief, loss, and trauma.

My spiritual journey led me to my own personal practice of walking meditation. It is hard to believe, but I thought I had discovered something new!

After a time, I learned that walking meditation was an art form brought to the modern Western world by a Buddhist monk named Thich Nhat Hanh. I read some of his books and used some of his ideas in my work, writing, and living. Then one day, I found a new book, *Walking Meditation* by Nguyen Anh-Huong and Thich Nhat Hanh.[1] The text was so rich and real that I knew I had to put my experiences and expertise on paper. I wanted to share them, as well as various emotional-spiritual self-help exercises, with my clients who were developing stress-management skills and who needed therapeutic self-help information to enrich their wholeness journeys.

I am happy when I feel connected to the energy of love. It is the universal life force flowing through each of us and through the totality of our planet and creation. The mindfulness practices within this book allow me, to the best of my ability, to engage and maintain a conscious connection to this energy. I have a passion for sharing what I've learned because the practices allow each of us to walk the pathways that lead to a higher quality of life. In turn, this leads to an increased quality of life for humankind as a whole.

Not all of us are born within nurturing families. Many of us are not exposed to a religious or spiritual environment that provides conscious access to information gained through regular spiritual practice. Because we are all learning, it is important for each of us to share the information we are

[1] Nguyen Anh-Huong and Thich Nhat Hanh, *Walking Meditation* (Boulder, CO: Sounds True, Inc., 2006).

given via the pathways of our own journeys. I live by the following principle: My thoughts and my life force energy are a part of universal wisdom and the light within.

Because I am part of the universal whole, my joyful and compassionate energy, as well as my angry, frustrated, and hurtful energy, become part of that whole. Each of us has a responsibility to nurture and grow positive energy and virtues. Our individual growth allows us to prosper intellectually, emotionally, and spiritually, as a collective. The only real goal in life is to learn what love is and share it with others.

This book was written as if you and I are sitting in a small class, learning together. I have chosen this intimate style because the information I will share relates to the development of our spiritual natures and our awakening to the meaning of our life. Our awakening leads us to become compassionate, loving, and contributing citizens of planet Earth.

I hope *Pathways to Wholeness* assists your spiritual healing journey and that you find joy within your experiences.

I wish you peace and wholeness.

—Janet G. Nestor

Part One

CONCEPTS TO ASSIST OUR JOURNEYS

Credit: William Recinos

Credit: Anastasiia Maalai

THE HOW-TO OF
MINDFULNESS

Though no one can go back and make a brand-new start,
anyone can start from now and make a brand-new ending.
—*James R. Sherman*[2]

Simply defined, *mindfulness* means being attentive and aware in a now-focused, experiential, and evaluative but not critical manner. Mindful, conscious thinking determines our overall satisfaction with life and our sense of well-being. Our thoughts are our personal construction crew. We construct our life one thought at a time.

The result of mindful awareness is the development of our heart virtues, which are definitions of love that become the basic positive building blocks of our lives. Some of the primary virtues are joy, happiness, kindness, compassion, and gratitude.

In the beginning, we apply mindfulness to one activity at a time until we get the hang of it. With practice, our applications gradually become a mindful lifestyle rather

---

[2] James R. Sherman, *Rejection: How to Survive Rejection and Promote Acceptance* (Golden Valley, MN: Pathway Books, 1982).

than a series of mindfulness activities. Below, you'll read two very different examples. The first is a step-by-step approach, and the second is an example of what it might feel like to apply mindfulness to an enjoyable life endeavor.

EXAMPLE 1

Our Ultimate Goal Is to Be Fully Present for Our Lives. It Takes Practice.

By practicing the art of mindfulness (being fully present) we become aware of all that is shaping our conscious perceptions: body sensations, feelings, emotions, thoughts, mental imagery, our immediate environment, and our history.

Our first step is to become aware of ourselves becoming aware. As we become aware of ourselves becoming aware, our perceptions expand to include the *wholeness* of who we are and our connection to universal oneness.

Our second step is to accept what already exists. What exists now is the reality in our life and consciousness. If we don't like what exists now, we are free to change it or change our perception of it. Letting our reality, as it is at this moment, be OK, no matter what that reality is like, is our third step.

Our fourth step is to realize that regardless of our reality, we are limitless and free.

Our fifth and final step is to allow our mind to become unencumbered—still, quiet, and peaceful. The result is a soft, calm, relaxed, reality-based communication and focus.

The mindfulness process can be applied to every aspect and activity of your life without exception. Success increases when you know which mindfulness skills are the most useful in achieving peace, tranquility, joy, and contentment. Your body believes everything that you say,[3] so make sure your self-talk is clear and to the point so your body can respond in a way that facilitates your personal growth. Here are some examples of clear mindfulness-based objectives:

- To adopt a more centered and grounded lifestyle
- To learn as much as I can and begin to apply the skills
- To quiet my racing, fearful, and worried mind
- To create inner peacefulness

EXAMPLE 2

The Rosebush—Mindful Gardening

If we are mindful (fully aware) of the beauty and health of our newly purchased rosebush, we carefully attend to it so that it can be planted, root, mature, and thrive. We plant the rosebush in a way that is mutually beneficial to the rosebush, ourselves, the environment surrounding the bush, and the environment of our homes and beyond. We become family to the rosebush that now lives within our care. We are partners in an interconnection that reflects the interdependence that exists between human beings and all the various forms of life within the natural world.

---

[3] Based on Barbara Hoberman Levine's *Your Body Believes Every Word That You Say: The Language of the Body/Mind Connection* (Fairfield, CT: WordsWork Press, 2000).

Compatibility of All Living Things

Once we have chosen a location that provides good rich soil and the necessary amount of sunlight, we continue our evaluation. We ask if this location enhances the beauty of the rosebush and maintains or enhances the beauty and design of the garden. If the answer is yes to all the above, we plant and begin to tend to the bush.

We make sure our new rosebush gets watered when the soil becomes dry and that it is fed with plant food, if needed. We monitor the contentment and the stress levels of the rosebush as it takes root and begins to grow. If signs of stress arise, we do our best to alleviate the stress. We notice new leaves when they appear, being aware that the new leaves are a lighter shade of green than the older leaves. We note the gradual change in them as they become mature. We notice the texture and shape of the leaves, and we know instantly, through subtle changes, if the new bush needs any special attention.

We are aware of the tight, green, little rosebuds when they first appear, and we watch their gradual unfolding as more and more of the colorful rose petals come into view. We celebrate the first full fragrant bloom, the rich color it contributes to the garden, and the pleasure it gives us. We look forward to each day and await subsequent blooms that will fill the air with their sweet scent. The old blooms are pruned gently and carefully, as needed.

Positive and Loving Life Energy Flows through All That Exists

Because of our conscious tending of the bush, we notice that we have become emotionally attached to the rosebush. The beauty of the bush and its successful growing season have nurtured us and provided pleasure and joy. Our joy is contagious, and we feel emotionally lighter. Our work seems easier and more satisfying. As our awareness expands, we realize that our life is more peaceful and pleasurable because we have been positively focused and fully present for a growing season.

Because of our mindful state, created through daily focused care and attention to the new rosebush, we are cognizant of a mutual sharing. Sharing exists between ourselves, the rosebush, the garden that supported the rose, and creation that provided sunlight, rain, and food for the bush. The rosebush is thriving, and because we have been fully present, so are we!

A Mindfulness Chain

A mindfulness chain is a positive and aware thought process that takes us into higher and higher states of insight and awareness. The ultimate goal is self-knowledge and enlightenment. The next section is an example of a chain, written to illustrate mindful reading. Notice how this mindfulness chain emphasizes the positive adaptations that occur when we read thoughtfully and mindfully and that allow one positive thought to lead us to another beneficial, insightful thought.

Mindful Reading

1. Awareness of the "feel" of the book as we examine it
2. Thoughtful exploration of the words, passages, and chapters of the book in an attempt to understand the author's intent
3. Noticing the emotional tone and feel of the words and passages
4. Conscious examination or meditation on chosen words and passages
5. Silent questioning
6. Increased insight and understanding
7. Healing, inspiration, and hopefulness
8. Higher levels of awareness
9. Changes in perceptions and beliefs
10. Different approaches and behaviors
11. Higher degree of satisfaction with self and life
12. A more peaceful inner nature
13. Spiritual awareness and awakening

What Is a Virtue?

The development of a virtue is a mindfulness practice and, at the same time, virtue development is the result of a daily mindfulness practice. The greater our focus, the more positive our life becomes.

The concept of virtue comes from ancient Taoist philosophy and permeates the study of tai chi, traditional Chinese medicine, and Eastern spiritual wisdom. The ideas were taught by the Chinese teacher and philosopher Lao Tzu, by the teacher Buddha and, later, by the teacher Christ. In our Western society and in our study of philosophy and personality, we might call a virtue a positive personality trait or a positive personal attribute—or heart-centered living.

Christians connect emotionally to the idea and formation of virtue. Christ used the concept over and over. In the New Testament book of Matthew, verses 4 and 5, he mentioned these virtues: obedience, teaching, healing, humility, comfort, satisfaction, mercy, purity, earnestness, goodness, reconciliation, strength, prayer, love, and friendship. A more detailed list of virtues is found in the "List of Virtues" in part 5 of this book.

How do we develop these virtues and gather the positive traits into our heart and mind? How do they become conscious parts of our inner core? And how does our positive inner core then determine our decisions and actions?

There are various names for the inner core. I began using the name *inner oasis* because of the mental picture of a lush, replenishing, supportive environment that supplies the needs of those who come to be nourished. In 2003 my colleagues and I named our office the Center of Well-Being because the words describe the perfect center that we all have that is wise, healthy, joyous, and peaceful. That center, that beautiful inner oasis, is the soul.

Below are three basic steps in the development of virtue:

1. We come to understand that the development of virtue is the development of our positive, spiritual inner nature. As we begin a spiritual journey, we eventually create a conscious lifestyle.
2. We adopt a spiritual path that leads to the expansion of our heart energy. Then we begin to respond to life from that energy, which is pure unconditional love.

3. We recognize that the development of virtue is not a cognitive or intellectual experience but something that we come to know and experience as a result of our chosen spiritual practice and journey. Our experiences then become our greatest teacher.

What Is Positive Mindful Thought?

Researchers say we have over six thousand thoughts each day. With all those thoughts, how do we know that our thoughts are positive?

All positive thought is based on the principles of unconditional love and, by definition, contains the following ingredients:

1. Positive intention
2. Positive content
3. Positive outcome for self, others, and all life

Why is positive thought important? A thought is pure energy and therefore has a life of its own. Once the thought is formed, it drifts into an unseen current and becomes part of a universal collective of thought that affects life not only today but throughout all time. If you think about all the thoughts that have been created since the birth of humankind, it is easy to see how collective thought is so ingrained with negativity.

The best way I know to explain the impact of negative thought is to share a dream with you. It is not about the collective thought of humankind. It is about the effect of positive thought on each of us. My dream was spiritual instruction concerning my life. It was visual and dynamic and is self-explanatory as well as thought-provoking. I leave you to create your own use for the wisdom you find within the dream.

I woke up after a dream this morning with an entirely different understanding of the essential nature of positive thought. The dream was about the fundamental building blocks of our lives—positive thought.

I experienced a small brick structure, maybe a square or a pyramid, being built, then crumbling, and then being rebuilt. This chain of events happened three times. I watched the first structure being built. One brick after another floated over and settled into place, and the small structure took shape. Before the structure was completed, it started to decay and crumble from the bottom up. Then it caved in upon itself. I thought (or maybe I was told silently) that those bricks were negative bricks. I experienced only focus and clarity as I watched. There was no emotion. I was a witness to an event. I was being taught.

Then the second structure was built in the same way. I saw no hands or people placing the bricks. The bricks just began forming a structure. This time, the bricks were different. Some had a negative charge. Some represented neutral thoughts. Other bricks represented mild to moderately positive thoughts. There was an occasional positive brick. Just like the first structure, it began to crumble from the foundation up, crumbling in on itself, before it was completed. Some bricks just broke apart. Others turned a powdery white color, softened, and crumbled.

Once again, the bricks began to form a structure. This time, the bricks were all positive bricks created by positive thoughts. As the bricks were placed and the structure began to take shape, it appeared solid and strong. For the first time, the structure was completed. The corners of the structure were sharp because the bricks fit together perfectly. It stood there—just a small, brick structure with a nice solid shape, perfectly formed. I thought, *This is solid and strong, and it is going to remain solid and strong. It will endure. It is a positive structure made from positive thought.*

I knew instinctively that the structures being built were me. Each brick that fell into place and formed each of the structures represented one of my thoughts—a part of me. I am the solid and enduring structure that thoughts created, and the solid structure was me. I was allowed to experience being it.

The negative bricks caused decay and destruction. The neutral ones were not strong enough to prevent the demise of the structure (me). I was given the understanding that success and permanence only come from building everything from the ground up with bricks of essential positive thought. Bricks of essential positive thought are a beautiful red-brick color, solid and strong. They stay solid and strong, even when the elements in the environment are negative and destructive.

My understanding of positive thought and energy went from intellectual to experiential because the dream was an experiential dream. I now have gut-level knowledge. I felt the communicated wisdom in my entire self, in every cell. The bricks represented *my* thoughts. The structures built were representative of *my* body. I am strong *only* when I am positive. I saw this. I now understand how important positivity is and how it influences the body.

As I lay in bed, appreciating the gift I was given, I realized how profound this message was. I felt and experienced the message in my heart, mind, and body. I was meant to grow and learn. I understood some of the highly personal reasons the experience was given to me. Other intentions, I have yet to discover.

While I have always thought of myself as a positive person, I came away from the dream with the understanding that some of my basic constructs aren't so positive after all. In fact, I realized that I had some recovery to do. If something is positive for me, it is a basic spiritual principle. It represents the expression of pure, unconditional love. It reflects the perfect wholeness of the divine intention for my life. The more positive my thought, my behavior, and my decisions, the closer I am to my divine purpose.

These principles hold true for everyone. The more positive you are, the closer you are to living authentically and in harmony with your divine purpose.

Dream for a moment. What would the world look like if each of us lived one day at a time, filled with positive thoughts? What if our body was built with positivity, and it. remained solid and strong throughout our lives?

Part Two
THE ORIGINAL WALK

Credit: Taylor

Credit: Karsten Winegeart

INTRODUCTION TO WALKING MEDITATION— JANET-STYLE

Peace and happiness are found where we are now, in the breath we take now. Real relaxation and peace happen when the past falls away, the future falls away, we stop our racing minds, and we walk into our own inner silence.

Walking meditation is a practice that can facilitate an awakening to the awareness that joy is within each of us all the time. We learn we can touch joy at any moment we choose to touch it. We no longer believe joy is an occasional event that happens by some random and lucky circumstance. We know where to find joy. Because we know joy is an innate part of us, we are comforted and able to trust.

I began practicing walking meditation long before I knew of Thich Nhat Hanh, the Vietnam-born Buddhist monk who is the modern-day father of this ancient healing art form. My personal practice grew out of my love of tai chi and the practice of conscious walking.

During my morning walks, I began to practice tai chi walking. Doing so shifted my focus from a walk for exercise to a kind of walk that was not only physically refreshing and strengthening but also emotionally and spiritually renewing. As I continued to practice, I developed a style of walking meditation that I used to strengthen my body, heal my spirit, and change my life.

Walking Meditation

When I began practicing walking as a form of meditation, I was very focused on understanding and developing my own flow of chi (energy). Moving meditation suited me perfectly. I walked my dog in the mornings and took much longer walks with her in a wooded area on weekends. Combining walking meditation with walking my beloved Dalmatian, Petie, seemed like a perfect idea and an exciting opportunity for companionship, personal growth, and healing.

Listed below are the directions for walking meditation that I devised for myself. This walking meditation practice strengthened my spiritual journey, helped me open and expand my definition and perception of love, and strengthened my relationship with nature and with myself. I felt more secure and safe. I was able to work on my breathing, which was a deep physical health issue due to allergies. I was not combining my stepping with my flow of breath at the time, but walking to increase my breathing capacity, which in turn helped me to soften and relax my body.

Directions for Walking Meditation—Janet-Style

1. Create an intention for the walk. The various intentions I created for my walks are similar to these:

    - To feel content and at peace at the completion of the walk
    - To feel more deeply connected to myself and creation
    - To experience a peaceful flow of energy during the walk
    - To be in the present moment, letting go of the past and the future
    - To embrace and honor nature and her healing qualities
    - To softly increase my physical endurance

2. Stand quietly in *wu-chi* (emptiness) at the beginning of the walk. We stand in this way until we feel grounded and connected to self and nature. To do this, we stand with our feet about shoulder-width apart, with weight evenly distributed between each foot, knees slightly bent, back straight, hips tucked in, and neck aligned with the spine. Our chin is slightly tucked so that our neck is straight.

    Our eyes have a soft focus. We breathe evenly and deeply, visualizing the breath as a silken stream. We allow ourselves to feel rooted into the ground, perhaps by visualizing roots growing from the bottoms of our feet into the earth. We give thanks to the strength of Earth and to the strength within ourselves. As we stand, we check in with ourselves, observe and note any aches and pains, and observe and make note of our general state of well-being. Once noted, we relax and enjoy simply being present with creation and ourselves. When we are content in the present moment, with mind quiet and spirit grateful for our connection to the universal energy flow that exists between all things, we begin to walk and fully enjoy our opportunities for mutual sharing.

3. We use the act of walking for focus. We notice our footsteps as they touch the earth. We allow ourselves to become energetically aware of each step, the feeling of each step, and how our body moves through each step. The noticing allows our mind to stay in the now and keeps our mind from reliving the past or "pre-living" the future. There is no problem-solving during this walk. We notice only our steps and our body, ease of movement, and the comfort and quality of our breathing. The secondary benefit of our focus is an increasingly more positive relationship with our body and the body's function.

4. Use the walk to connect with nature. There is great solace in the healing power of nature. Make friends with her. Notice new growth. Notice the sounds and smells and the life force of nature. Notice the blossoms, the foliage, and the animals that come into view. I made friends with a particularly large old pine tree. I stopped by to physically touch her and speak to her each time I walked. Her presence was particularly healing for me. I hope my appreciation helped her quality of life as much as she helped mine. I asked her if I could have a small piece of her magnificent old bark to carry with me. I placed it in my car to remind me of what is possible

and to encourage my inward focus and connection to all that is.

5. We walk until we are at the end of our walk and then return to our starting location. Our inner being tells us when to return to the starting point.

6. At the end of the walk, we stand in *wu-chi*. We check in to see if we have achieved our intention. The check-in is not a pass or fail but a noticing that provides insight. Has the walk helped to increase our feeling of well-being and our sense of connection to self and life? How do we feel physically in comparison to how we felt at the start of the walk? Does our focus on our breath and the walk quiet our mental chatter?

    Each of us has the opportunity to glimpse the depth of loving insight and experience of wholeness that is available through a regular practice of meditation. Any restorative, awakening practice is an ongoing process. Our awareness increases, a step at a time, and continues as long as we practice. Each day, a new pathway of understanding opens to us, and each of us has our own special window of experience that is important for our growth. Meditation has a way of providing exactly what we need.

Credit: Philip Myrtrop

AS I WALK, I AM

Earth is my home.
Her foliage brings softness and beauty,
and provides the breath of life.
Everything about her brings attention to divine beginning.

My footsteps touch her peacefully, and I know.
My eyes gently focus on everything and nothing, and I see.

My mind is quiet and free of worry, and it refreshes me.
My breath flows softly in and out, and
my senses are heightened.

My body is alive, as I fully experience my wholeness
and the miraculous nature of each footstep.

My awareness is expanded, and I acknowledge
and honor the Presence within me.

My being merges with all that there is, and I am at home.

My totality celebrates life.
Creation is a part of me, and I am a part of her.

As I Walk, I Am

Part Three

ENRICHING THE JOURNEY

Credit: Pratap Chhetr

The content in "Enriching the Journey" is an integration of "Walking Meditation—Janet-Style," my professional training, the wisdom derived from my spiritual journey, and the beautiful wisdom contained in Nguyen Anh-Huong and Thich Nhat Hanh's 2006 book, *Walking Meditation*, published by Sounds True, Inc. (www.soundstrue.com).

Credit: Ale Romo

MINDFUL BREATHING: RESTING ON THE BREATH OF LIFE

Learn to smile in the sweet way of a child. A smile from the soul is spiritual relaxation. A real smile is a thing of true beauty, the artistic work of the 'Inner Ruler Immortal' ... Affirm before taking up the work for the day—'Within me there is a perfect form—the form Divine. I am now all that I desire to be! I visualize daily my beautiful being until I breathe it into expression!'

—Emil [4]

I was taught by example to take breathing for granted. I remember the childhood contests that determined which of us could dip underwater and hold our breath for the longest count. Some of us learned to regulate our breathing when we took swimming lessons. The singers among us were taught intentional breath control to strengthen our lungs and enhance our vocal performances. Most of us were

---

[4] Baird T. Spalding, *Life and Teaching of the Masters of the Far East*, Vol. 1 (Marina del Rey, CA: DeVorss & Company, 1924).

not engaged in disciplines that required us to focus on our breath or to increase our lung capacity.

Our breathing was unconscious, automatic, and often shallow. Today, as adults, we can go for hours at a time, preoccupied with the business of life, and fail to experience one conscious breath. Only when we undergo some sort of stress that disrupts our breathing rhythm do we become conscious of our breathing abilities. A run in the park, sudden shock, fear, a sneeze, or something more serious, like choking, can get our attention and cause us to concentrate on our breathing—for as long as it takes to feel better.

Mindful breathing is the direct opposite of unconscious breathing because we choose to notice our breathing and the quality of our in-and-out breath. We fully experience each in-and-out-breath. We are aware that we can exercise some control over the length and depth of each breath. We can enjoy our breathing and derive comfort in its steadiness and fullness. We notice the calming in-and-out flow and are aware of the rise and fall of our abdomen. Our awareness is an inward experience. We notice our inner state of being, the comfort of the breath, the comfort level of our body, our emotional ease or "dis-ease," and our emotions and their impact on our physical body and spirit body. If we touch deeply enough, we notice the inner constancy and peacefulness of a deep, eternal connection within. This connection can be referred to as higher consciousness, universal wisdom, and other names, such as God consciousness.

Mindful Breathing Is an Energetic Healing Art

Mindful breathing is a healing art form in its own right. It is an integral part of walking meditation, as taught by Nguyen Anh-Huong and Thich Nhat Hanh in their 2006 book, *Walking Meditation*. When using their style of this ancient technique, it is important that we learn the art of mindful breathing before we begin the practice of walking meditation.

Mindful breathing can be practiced anywhere because we breathe everywhere. Our sitting or standing positions and locations are secondary to the process.

Our goal is relaxation and the ability to maintain inner calm when our life situation is hectic and stress-filled. We seek to soften our response to life, soften our muscles, quiet our racing mind, and touch the peace and compassion within. Mindful, focused breathing creates a pathway that leads to the expansion of our naturally peaceful inner nature and the intentional creation of a soothing external environment.

Mindful breathing is possible for almost anyone, regardless of physically challenging conditions or state of health. Even if our breathing is impaired due to allergies, asthma, or other illnesses, we can practice breathing as a form of comfort and relaxation. We only need a willingness to breathe consciously. This includes a willingness to allow the time required to accomplish our goals, readiness to move deeply within, and a yearning for increased mental, emotional, physical, and spiritual well-being.

When we are deeply calm and feel safe in the meditative relaxation of mindful breathing, our self-awareness expands. We become increasingly more conscious of our hidden beliefs and perceptions. We can suddenly become aware of and release buried negative emotions or become aware of the many positive emotions tucked within.

Increased awareness and release are profoundly restorative and regenerative when we are ready to understand and feel. When we are not ready to look toward our emotions and greet them with love and compassion, they can feel overwhelming, regardless of their content. Positive emotions, such as joy, love, and compassion, can overwhelm us with such gratitude and relief that we feel washed out or become temporarily immobilized. Because all of us long to experience positive and affirming emotions, their absence can be profoundly disturbing. When we feel such emotions without warning, some of us will respond to them in much the same way as we respond to negatively perceived emotions.

Mindful Breathing Allows Us to Access Our Unconscious Emotions

I first experienced a burst of unwanted emotion during a resting meditation when I lived in Moraga, California. It was a warm, sunny morning, and I was on my patio, reclining on a lounge chair, very deep in an imagery-filled breathing exercise. All of a sudden, a burst of red-hot anger caused me to jump out of my chair in stunned shock. I had been so peaceful and had no idea, at the time, that deeply buried emotion could surface during a meditation. I certainly had no idea that extreme anger—so strong that it moved my body—was hidden within.

Our emotions are a part of us, much the same as our arms are a part of us. In mindful breathing, we open our heart and arms and welcome all our emotions with a soft embrace and a gentle, loving smile. Because of our welcoming embrace and our acceptance and willingness, our emotions feel comfortable with us, and our comfort with the emotions enables us to allow them to stay. When they stay, emotional, physical, and spiritual healing occurs.

When there are too many conflicted and painful emotions arising at one time, however, feelings of overwhelm and strong stress-related symptoms can occur during the meditative experience. If this is a possibility, it is necessary to postpone mindful breathing until a greater level of healing is accomplished. If we are working with a health care professional who is trained to facilitate mindful breathing, we can ask for help and perhaps practice our skills during our sessions.

Sometimes, intense emotions will arise, and even though we perceive them as unpleasant, we know that we can handle them. We are ready to approach them, accept them, and let them flow. Emotional flow results as we clear the difficult, challenging emotions and heal our wounded spirit.

You might want to try this imagery: Scan your body and identify the areas of your body that hold a difficult emotion. Visualize a river that will lovingly carry the emotion away from the point(s) of stress. Then, imagine the positive physical and emotional impact as each emotion flows from your body on the wings of the water.

Instructions for working through overwhelming emotional experiences are included within the context of the following instructions for mindful breathing:

Instructions for Mindful Breathing

- Ideally, our external environment is quiet and restful.
- Find a position that is comfortable, whether standing, reclining, or sitting.
- We can change our position until we find comfort. Wear comfortable clothing.
- We keep our head and neck aligned with our spinal column. If we are sitting or standing, our chin is slightly tucked so the back of our neck is aligned with our spine; if reclining, we use a thin pillow so that we can maintain the neck alignment.
- Our eyes are closed, or our vision is softly focused, with our eyes seeing nothing in particular.
- We relax our shoulders and continue to allow them to soften as we breathe.
- We loosen our arms, elbows, wrists, and fingers by shaking out our hands and wrists until they feel alive.
- We rest our hands on our abdomen or along the sides of our body.
- We allow our face to relax. We open and close our mouth and yawn to stretch our face because it feels good and softens our muscles.
- We relax our eyes by opening and closing them several times and by maintaining a soft focus.
- A soft, gentle smile is our catalyst for creating an inner relaxation and peacefulness.
- We notice our breath flowing in and out like a gentle breeze that softly caresses and comforts us.
- When we are completely ready and settled into our position, we rest our hands on our lower abdomen to help us monitor our breathing.

- We take an in-breath and allow it to fall to our belly on the exhale and settle there. Then we begin breathing in and out from our belly.

- As we breathe in, we rest on our breath and silently repeat a meaningful word, such as *resting, relaxing,* or *soothing.*

- As we breathe out, we rest on our breath and silently repeat a meaningful word, such as *softening, comforting,* or *lightening.* (I like to say, "resting—softening," "relaxing—lightening," or "soothing—comforting," spoken in pairs.)

- We breathe, repeating our meaningful words until we feel we are done.

- If powerful emotions arise during our mindful breathing, and we feel safe in the meditation, we invite the emotions to stay with us. We ask them to rest beside us while we continue to breathe from our belly in a smooth, gentle flow of breath. We see our breath flowing through the emotion and creating change that allows the emotion to open and flow freely through us and away from us. Our regular, deep breathing has the ability to dissolve the troubling emotion. If the emotions of deep love, peace, and compassion arise, we welcome them with our smiles. If we feel ready to have them become part of us, we invite them into our heart.

The following methods of mindful breathing might be more helpful to some who are not comfortable with the directions above. The second alternative method works particularly well if we want to intentionally prepare to match our breath to our steps, as we are instructed to do in breath walking, a style of walking meditation that we will discuss in the next part of the book.

Alternative Mindful Breathing 1

- Follow the directions as written above. When we are ready, we begin to breathe from our belly.
- We focus on the in-breath and the out-breath.
- After a few moments of quiet breathing, we use counting to strengthen our focus.
- We count from one to ten, using *one* on the in-breath, *two* on the out-breath, *three* on the in-breath, and *four* on the out-breath. We continue in this way through ten.
- When we take the tenth breath, we begin all over again, starting at one and breathing our way to ten.
- We continue to breathe in this way until we are deeply relaxed, our muscles are softened, and our mind is restful and focused on the breath.
- We continue to breathe in this manner until we are ready to return to waking external consciousness. (A fifteen-minute session is an ideal time for most people.)

Alternative Mindful Breathing 2

Some people find it more helpful to use the same pattern that we use in the breath walk. On the in-breath we count one, two, three, and on the out-breath we count one, two, three or extend it to one, two, three, four, five to obtain a deep and soothing longer breath. The counting measures our breath and helps us create a comforting rhythm that is right for us. I like this method because I like regulating the length of my breath. I feel that I empty my lungs more efficiently using this method. A fifteen-minute session is ideal.

Alternative Mindful Breathing 1 works very well as a short, ten-breath *qigong* when we are in acute stress. It is also a means of bringing mindful breathing into our daily lives. *Qigong* is a word from traditional Chinese medicine that can be translated to mean a breathing exercise or physical movement that creates relaxation.

We can breathe ten meditative breaths while stopped at a traffic light, while sitting in a stressful meeting, before public speaking, or while waiting for a doctor's appointment. I teach my clients who experience anxiety and panic to use the ten-breath *qigong* as a means of monitoring and maintaining an acceptable level of relaxation.

Mindful meditative breathing is a powerful healing practice and is perfect to help with calming a chattering mind. It is a wonderful way to prepare for the day ahead or settle down for a night of good sleep. It can serve us as an alternative to walking meditation when we are injured, are too sick to walk, are recovering from surgery, or have a physical challenge that prohibits walking. If we find ourselves in one of these circumstances, it is good to try the various methods of mindful breathing and choose one that meets our physical, emotional, and spiritual needs. All the methods work equally well; they exercise our lungs and help us heal.

If we use mindful breathing in the same way we use meditative walking, we can silently speak words or phrases that allow a particular kind of healing. For example, we might want to think *healing* on the in-breath and *now* on the out-breath, or *wisdom* on the in-breath and *shared* on the out-breath. We can choose pairs of words that gather to us the virtues that we need at the moment. If we are in need of peace and comfort, we mentally speak *peaceful* on the in-breath and *comforting* on the out-breath. Other pairs of words that we might meditate with are wisdom/now, calmness/clarity, and joyous/connection. To lengthen our breaths, we might want to try something like "I welcome the day" on the in-breath, and "I am grateful today" on the out-breath. If we have been going through a very stressful life event, we might choose "I am safe today" on the in-breath, and "I am strong today" on the out-breath. We choose the words that feed our soul, calm our mind, and fill our heart with the exact feelings we need for healing.

Mindful breathing helps us balance our autonomic nervous system, regulate our heart rate, and maintain a relaxed, calm, and clear mindful state that is now focused and fully present. The result is a return to self: a richer, calmer, happier, more contented, reality-based life. It simply takes a regular practice to create the positive changes that we desire.

Credit: Norbert Braun

PATHWAYS COMBINE:
A MINDFUL APPROACH

A journey of a thousand miles begins with a single step.
—Lao Tzu[5]

Life is a journey. We share our journey with family, friends, work associates, spiritual friends, and many professional helpers. Our journey is also shared, consciously and unconsciously, with various organizations and institutions that exist within our local, national, and world communities. Even if we don't realize it, life is a broad and profound voyage shared with every living being on the planet and with the living bioenergetic system of planet Earth. Earth provides, directly or indirectly, everything we need to sustain all forms of life.

As our world civilizations have evolved from rural agrarian communities into industrial and technological societies, we have become increasingly distanced from our innate inner nature. We miss the simple pleasures and realities of life.

---

[5] Lao Tzu, *Complete Works of Lao Tzu*, translated by Hua-Ching Ni (Santa Monica: Seven Star Publications Group, 1979).

There are professionals to help us do almost anything. Doctors and nurses take care of us when we are sick, help us in times of serious illness and death, and facilitate the birth of our babies. Professionals manage our money and take care of it in banks. Commercial farms plant and grow our food. Others manufacture our clothing, build our homes, help us find jobs, clean our houses, and maintain our lawns and gardens. We can even call someone to go to the pharmacy or grocery store for us, and they will deliver everything right to our door. We are distanced, emotionally and physically, from the basics of life: the miracle of a garden sprouting little green leaves from vegetable seeds; the joy of harvesting a field of potatoes or picking apples from an orchard full of fresh fruit; the taste of fresh, warm milk straight from a cow; the birth of a colt and the sight of it standing in the first minutes of life to nurse from its mother; the simplicity of having a cup of fresh, cold water from an underground spring. It is not surprising that many of us do not have a personal relationship with our magnificent Earth home. We do not even have conscious awareness that a personal relationship with Earth and all of creation is possible.

Like many of us, Earth is ailing and feels alone in her struggles. We have ignored her needs for so long that she is suffering from our carelessness, and her ability to function is threatened. She needs us to care for her, love her, and nourish her so that she can maintain the ability to sustain us. Walking meditation is one of the positive healing pathways we can take for ourselves and those we love, and this includes the nonhuman citizens of the world and Earth herself.

In the beginning, we practice walking meditation because we want to try something new and because it is a peaceful, harmonious, spiritual practice. It facilitates higher levels of inner awareness and deep relaxation. We learn self-acceptance, to be at home within ourselves, and to enjoy the experience of conscious, mindful being. We learn to stop our racing minds, relax, embrace joy, and become fully present.

Eventually, we practice walking meditation because it is a gentle, spiritual pathway to gratitude, balance, and feelings of personal solidarity and safety. Because of our practice, we learn to live within the energy of love. Within that love, we find a lifestyle that is inclusive and welcoming.

With Each Step, We Leave Our Energetic Footprint

When we walk in our usual unconscious way, our mind is full of the business of life—past, present, and future. As we walk unconsciously, we carry our worries and woes along with us and often attempt to dump our anxieties, concerns, and sorrows along the way. With each step of our unconscious walk, our mind wanders from topic to topic. We use our walks to chat with a friend, talk on our cell phones, plan our days, worry about our families, or work though fears and life stressors.

With unconscious intent, we leave behind the energy of our fear, anger, and frustration. We are unaware that the negative energy and stress dispersed without conscious thought have become a burden to Earth and to all other people who spend time walking where we have walked.

When we walk consciously and mindfully, the opposite result is obtained—we add positivity to our internal and external environments. As we walk in joy, compassion, and peace, with the purpose of deepening our connection to our own inner beings, we create a consciousness of these virtues for ourselves, for Earth, and for other people to experience and enjoy as they walk where we have walked.

We Feel Emotions Long after We Have Vibrated with Them

If we use the metaphor of drawing a line through water, it is easy to see our impact on others. Instantly, the line is there, and then it is not. Yet the ripples along the line vibrate out from it for as far as the eye can see. And they continue on, becoming part of the water.

Drawing the line affected the water. The impact was felt long after the line was visible. This is what happens with our emotions. Their impact is present long after we have pushed those emotions out of our conscious minds. Everyone and everything we touch experiences the ripples of our emotions long after we have vibrated with them. Each individual life-form and inanimate object touched by our charged emotional state experiences, consciously or unconsciously, the ripple we created.

If our ripples are negative, our path and the environment around us become overloaded with our troubled emotions. These emotions become part of the experience of all living and inanimate things that share space with us. An emotional burden is created for our friends and family, the physical environment, and Earth herself. If our ripples are positive, we lighten our personal burdens, the burden of each life-form and inanimate object in our environment, and the burden of Earth herself.

When we walk mindfully, we simply walk for the enjoyment of the experience. We don't have a plan to arrive anywhere at any particular time or to walk at any particular speed. The environment, our health, our mood, and the walk itself determine our speed. Our destination is in each step, and each step is where we are now. This means that our attention is a focused inner awareness. We notice and experience our body's movements and each footstep as we take it.

During our walks, our past is past and no longer a part of our present. We don't daydream about what could have been, should have been, or might be tomorrow. We do not problem-solve or allow our thoughts to wander into a future that has not yet arrived. As we walk, we simply are where we are now—our mind focused on our steps and our breath—and we are peacefully present in our now. Each step and breath is now. Our mind and our heart are focused in the now.

Our Peaceful Inner Nature Is a Constant

Many of us have known depression, worry, loss, and feelings of being overwhelmed. Deep inside, we may believe that there is nothing for us other than what we usually experience and feel in our daily lives. We believe that our histories and our emotions define who we are now and limit who we can become. We feel trapped by the circumstances of our life and see no way to change them. We are so strongly identified with our details that we are overwhelmed by them. Some of us may think that death is the only solution.

Walking meditation helps us create an inner atmosphere that allows us to change our beliefs about who we are and about what is possible for us to learn and accomplish. As we walk mindfully in the now, leave behind our past, and stop pre-living our future, we gradually become conscious of our compassionate, joyous, and loving inner nature. We become aware of the creative universal life force flowing within us. This wisdom and our heightened awareness change everything. We now know that our inner nature is constant and that we have access to all of it, all of the time, because it is part of us. Our peaceful inner being is with us, no matter what is going on around us.

The more we walk mindfully in the here and the now, the more we are in contact with our quiet, peaceful, and restful inner nature. Our awareness allows us the freedom to trust and to be open to our authentic self and to the total experience of living. The more we walk mindfully, the more we feel in tune with ourselves, Earth, and all of creation. We feel at home and nurtured by nature and Earth.

We gradually learn that taking each step in peace and love is a metaphor for living each moment of each day in peace and love. Each step we take is taken now. Each breath we breathe is breathed now. Each experience we encounter is felt now. We learn that if peaceful, loving consciousness slips from our grasp, it is only a step and a breath away.

Sharing Our Experiences with Earth

As we mindfully take each step, we are aware of our body as it moves, and we are aware of the miracle of movement. In our meditative state of consciousness, we recognize and understand that Earth is a magnificent living organism, vibrating and pulsating with internal and external life. We are a part of her, and she is a part of us.

We know that because Earth is a living energy. We actively share the experience of our walks with her. As we consciously take each step, we are aware that our feet gently and lovingly massage Earth's surface. We notice our footprints. We are aware of the texture of our walking path and feel the pebbles press into Earth's surface. We realize that with each step, we are sharing our energies and blending them with the energy of Earth.

With each conscious step, Earth returns our loving touch. We feel the vibration of her caress on the soles of our feet and experience her energy nurturing our legs and spine. Because of our physical experience and her solidarity, each step feels emotionally safe and secure. With each healing step, we give gratitude for Earth's virtuous gifts of strength and permanence. We give gratitude for her wisdom and sensual beauty. With each step, Earth thanks us for our peaceful, companionable journey, our love and care.

We understand the mutuality, the deep sharing of all life-forms that exist upon and within Earth. This understanding enhances our awakening and sense of belonging.

Within our heart and mind, we have the seeds of all possible emotions, and each of these seeds has the potential to root, sprout, mature, and blossom. If we plant and water the negative seeds, they will sprout, mature, and blossom into powerful emotions that we perceive and experience as unpleasant and harmful. Our gardens will be filled with blossoms that pollinate our life with sadness, sorrow, grief, loss, and other emotions associated with stress and pain. If we plant and water our positive seeds—our virtues— they will sprout, mature, and blossom into emotions that we perceive and experience as positive. Our gardens will be pollinated with blossoms that spread pleasure, happiness, and love.

The practice of walking meditation and the loving gardens we have created and nurtured into full beauty allow us to be fully present and to feel confident and emotionally healthy. As healthy people, we welcome all emotions and allow them to flow through us, fully processing what we experience. Walking in peacefulness provides us a means to plow through and uproot negative thoughts and perceptions, process our emotions, heal our wounded heart, mend our broken spirit, and create balance and joy within and without.

Linking our stepping and breathing allows us to remain now-focused and enjoy our walks with a calm and peaceful mind. As our love, gratitude, and healing energy are shared with Earth, and Earth shares her healing strength and beauty with us, our awareness of the majesty of all life increases. As our awareness of our peaceful, loving inner nature increases, the negative impact of our hurried, stressful world seems to lessen. We find real joy in the simplicity of a bird's song, the gentleness of a breeze, a beautiful sunrise, or a radiantly colored sunset. The relaxation, quiet mind, and increased awareness that grow from walking meditation allow us to function at a higher emotional and intellectual level. Walking meditation supports increased clarity and insight. It promotes our ultimate goal of a healthier body and lifestyle.

We Develop a Positive Relationship between Mind, Body, and Spirit

Most of the time in normal workaday life, we find ourselves locked into emotional and behavioral patterns that become habitual, stagnant, and burdened. Unconsciously, we pass through life, unaware of our body, never really recognizing its needs. Because we are anxious or simply unaware, we breathe shallowly and never completely empty our lungs of the old, stale air that accumulates in them. We feel sluggish, agitated, and unhappy, and we don't know why. Walking meditation changes all of that. We become aware of our capacity to move, our lungs' capacity to inhale and exhale efficiently, and our ability to simply enjoy being alive in our body.

Gradually, we become aware of our body moving gracefully to a rhythm that we create—our steps attuned to our movements and our lungs filling and emptying with comfort in perfect harmony with our stepping. At this moment, we realize that we have developed a positive relationship with our body, our body's need to move and breathe, our spiritual-emotional self, our environment, nature, and Earth herself. We are content.

There are several focus options for walking meditation, and each focus guides our growth in a slightly different way. We choose our focus to meet the needs we have on any given day. Sometimes, we might want the simplicity of a breath walk. Nature walking, emotion walking, and health walking are explained in the next section. The benefits of each type of walking gradually become a natural part of our new mindfulness lifestyle. The sense of safety and connectedness finds its way into our attitudes and decision-making. We are infused with the wisdom derived from our practice. When all of this happens, we find we are living from our spiritual center—our center of well-being.

Credit: Nurhadi Cahyono

BREATH WALKING: MAINTAINING FOCUS WITH BREATH

Few of us ever consider how the nostrils of every living person pulse to their own rhythm, opening and closing like a flower in response to our moods, mental states, and perhaps even the sun and moon.

—James Nestor[6]

The idea of matching our steps with our breath is an idea taken from Nguyen Anh-Huong and Thich Nhat Hanh in *Walking Meditation.*

My first resting-meditation teacher introduced the idea of focused in-and-out breathing, coupled with a word that described an intuited need. When I began walking as a form of meditation, I concentrated on improving my breathing capacity, but I was not using breath as a focus for my walk.

When breath walking, counting or single words or phrases are silently spoken on the in-breath and out-breath to measure the length of each breath and as a way

---

[6] James Nestor, *Breath. The New Science of a Lost Art* (London: Penguin Life, 2020).

to sustain mindfulness. Increased physical, emotional, and spiritual awareness is achieved in the same way. The words and phrases serve as affirmations, and they support the development of our sense of self-worth and self-love.

Solid Mechanics: Heightened Energy Flow and Well-Being

We practice breath walking as we learn the mechanics of walking meditation. Conscious breathing, as we take each step, is the core skill that is the strength and power of walking mediation.

For some people, it is easier to begin their practice on a quiet indoor track. The quiet enhances focus. Others choose to practice in nature. They are more relaxed and focused in the outdoors

As we walk, we breathe through our nose and allow our breathing to relax our shoulders. Our neck is straight, and our head is aligned with our spine. We keep our eyes softly focused in a way that seems to allow us to see clearly, yet we focus on nothing in particular. Our chin is slightly tucked to maintain alignment, and we look forward and to the ground in a way that maintains alignment. We walk with our body in this posture to create a heightened energy flow. It helps us develop awareness and appreciation of the energy within our body.

Our focus is simultaneously an inward focus of heightened body awareness and an outward focus so that we can enjoy the sights, sounds, and scents of being alive. It is helpful to practice the posture and experience the feel of walking in the posture before we begin to match our breath with our steps.

If we have problems combining our steps and breath, we can use mental imagery to practice walking and breathing. Mental imagery amplifies the impact of any skill we are trying to learn. As we practice with our mind's eye, we improve our physical skills and receive the same soothing benefits as we would when walking on a track or on an outdoor path.

We can accomplish breath walking on an indoor track, walking down the driveway to pick up the morning paper, along a beautiful path in a wooded area, in the halls at work, in our local shopping mall, on a playground full of children, or on the battlefields of war. The place where we walk is insignificant to the process. We each can find a location that is just right for our needs. If we have trouble finding a location, we can simply blend walking meditation into our daily life by using the places that are available.

I live close to a natural habitat. A breath walk is always a pleasure. I can pause to visit with nature and enjoy the animals and birds in their natural environment. One morning while walking on the greenway near my home, I was delighted to see a beaver scampering along the side of the creek. He was trying to find a place to jump in for a swim. I had no idea that beavers lived along the creek and watching this one was an exciting surprise.

During another walk, a solitary wild duck came swooping down to make an almost silent landing on a pond near the path. I was close to the pond so watching him make flight adjustments and glide in for a flawless landing was a magnificent sight.

As we learn to coordinate our steps with our breath, we become more present during our walks. In the beginning, it may be easier simply to take an in-breath with the first step and an out-breath with the next step. In doing this, we focus on deep breathing from our belly, taking a naturally deep in-breath with one step and a complete out-breath with the next step. Sometimes, we can count one, two, three, four—breathing in on one, out on two, in on three, and out on four. We can speed up or slow down our stepping to accommodate the breath. We can repeat this over and over, breathing with natural deepness and stepping with a rhythm that we establish.

The beauty of walking, breathing, and counting to measure our breaths is our total concentration on breathing, counting, and walking. Holding our hands on our lower abdomen helps to establish the ability to breathe from our belly. We can easily feel the rise and fall of our breath.

Our Gentle Smile Provides Instant Relaxation

As our skills improve, we can add more steps to each breath. We can measure our breath and take two or three steps to an in-breath and two or three steps to an out-breath. The length of our breath depends on where we are walking, our level of health, and our lung capacity. We always respect the health requirements of our body. If we become tired or notice we are having difficulty breathing, we can alter our pattern to establish comfort. As we walk, we repeat our comfortable stepping and breathing over and over, remembering to soften our facial muscles with a gentle smile. The gentle smile is our greatest ally. Once we shape our mouth into a smile, the relaxation is instantly apparent.

Try it right now while you are reading. Close your eyes, and observe what happens to your mood and body as a result of a smile. I notice my response to my own smile. The muscles at the back of my neck relax, my shoulders soften, and I am more fully present and at peace.

Feeling Our Energy Flow through Our Body

I love the feeling of energy flowing through my hands as I walk. Knowing that my energy is flowing freely through my body exhilarates me. I walk with my fingers slightly open and my hands gently cupped, so I fully experience the energy.

Since we are all energy beings, each of us has the skill to feel our energy flowing through our body. Once we have established a rhythm to our stepping and breathing, we can easily focus on the tingling in our hands or the gentle warmth as the energy begins to flow from the energy center in the palm of each hand.

As we take our breath walks, it is advantageous to add silent words to the breaths and the steps. The words allow us to deepen our relaxation and create affirmative intent. We might say "calming" on the in-breath and "relaxing" on the out-breath. We might choose to refer to being fully present and at home in our body while we walk. We might say "present" on the in-breath and "now" on the out-breath. Or we could say "I am" on the in-breath and "fully present" on the out-breath. We can change our words to accommodate our stepping and breathing and the length and depth of the breaths. We might want to say "I am present now" as we breathe in and again as we breathe out. This phrase would be equivalent to counting one, two, three, four on the in-breath and one, two, three, four on the out-breath.

Intuitively, we know what we need. It is sometimes helpful to allow our words to change during our walks so that we create more than one affirming message. It is equally important to choose words that we are comfortable speaking. I may start my walk saying "I am at home," then switch to "I am at peace," and complete the walk by affirming "I am peacefully at home." Other options might be "I'm walking now" on the in-breath and "I'm breathing now" on the out-breath. "I am fully alive" is another option.

Credit: Karen Fedda

NATURE WALKING: CREATING FOCUS WITH BREATH AND NATURE

Thank you, Mother Nature, for all you teach us and for your patience while we learn to treat you with respect.[7]

My earliest years were spent living on a farm along a dirt road in rural West Virginia. From the back screened-in porch, I watched the Little Kanawha River flowing peacefully by. From the front porch, I could look to the left and see my grandfather's apple orchard. It produced the apples that turned into the apple butter I loved. If I stood in the lane by the garage, I could see the edge of the lush, deep, old-growth forest that gave way to the grazing area of the pasture field.

I grew up honoring and loving nature, the farm, and the fresh fruit and vegetables that my grandfather cultivated

---

[7] Janet G. Nestor, *Finding Nature's Magic* (Seattle: Kindle Direct Publishing, 2020).

there. Because of this, nature walking is my favorite style of walking.

Today, I restore myself by cocooning in the energy of the forest and by being near the sound of flowing water. Nature walking is the style of walking meditation that I developed for myself in 1996. I intertwine my experiences with the expert wisdom of Nguyen Anh-Huong and Thich Nhat Hanh in the information that we share together. Once again, we combine our in- and out-breaths with our steps and use silently spoken words to strengthen our focus.

We Bring the Innocence of Childhood to Walking Meditation

Babies are naturally present-moment-oriented. It is so easy to forget that they are pure spiritual beings when they take their first breath and enter the complexities of human life. Their physical, emotional, and spiritual needs are related to comfort and feeling safe and secure in the love of their caregivers. Walking in nature creates similar feelings of comfort and safety.

As babies, we found joy in the simplest of activities: a smile, a hug, the warmth of a bath. We squealed and laughed as we reached for our toys. We found pure joy in the sight of our mother's smiling face. As toddlers and preschoolers, we loved to play with brightly colored leaves as they floated on the breeze. We jumped in piles of them as our parents raked the yard. As children, we laughed in anticipation and wonder as we chased fireflies in the shadow of the setting sun. I remember rolling down the slope behind my grandparents' house until I was dizzy with laughter.

I loved watching my children climb the jungle gym. They laughed from their soul as they pumped their legs on the swings so they could scream as they felt the wind hit their faces and whip through their hair. As children, we greeted life with curiosity and openness, and our joyous laughter was the music of the day. As adults, we bring the spirit of our childhood innocence and joy to walking meditation.

Each walk is an adventure and an opportunity for something new. As we walk, the totality of our being awakens to the magnificence of the gift of life. These marvelous experiences are available to us simply because we are alive.

Standing like a Tree, Rooted and Grounded

Prior to our walk, we honor the strength and solidarity of Earth and the trees by standing in a *qigong* pose called "Standing like a Tree." We stand quietly and honor our flow of breath, our life, the solidarity of the earth under our feet, and the groundedness and rootedness of the trees. We stand with our back straight and our head straight above our shoulders, our neck aligned with our spine, and our feet shoulder-width apart. Our eyes look straight ahead and are softly focused. Our eyes are aware, yet the vision is soft and nonspecific.

We drop our shoulders so that they become soft and comfortable. We breathe in and out and allow our body to become quiet with relaxation. Our stance remains solid. First, we shift all of our weight to the right foot and feel that foot take root into the ground. Then, we shift all our weight to the left foot and feel our weight root the left foot solidly to the ground.

Once we experience this, we stand with our weight evenly distributed between our right and left feet. Our knees are slightly bent to allow the energy to flow through us, just as sap flows through a tree. We relax our elbows, wrists, and fingers as we stand. We feel the bubbling well—Kidney 1 Acupoint in Chinese medicine—on the soles of our feet as they touch the ground. This is the gateway for Earth's energy to enter the body. We give thanks for the life-giving energy and the solidness of the earth.

As we imagine being fully rooted and joined with Earth, we picture Earth supplying us with all the nourishment that we need. We stand, centered and quiet, giving gratitude to Earth. We allow ourselves to be nurtured until we are ready to begin our walk. Standing like a tree is very inspiring and edifying. We can stand in this way for as long as we choose to do so, finding comfort in our own being and in the strength of Earth.

During our walks, we sometimes are led to observe our environment and drink in the energy and beauty of a particular sight or sound. Our soul soars as we stand by a stream, listening to the water flowing, as the birds serenade from a distance. We might walk among a stand of trees that draws us into its midst for renewal. Perhaps our heart expands at the music of a waterfall that plunges majestically from a mountainside. We might find emotional healing as we meander through a field of wildflowers. Our senses might fill with awe as we enjoy a panoramic view from a mountaintop. There might be a feeling of wonder as we watch butterflies come to dine on the nectar provided by the blooms along our path. As we enjoy what is given so freely, we breathe deeply, and our calm, restful breath heightens our experience.

As we walk, we become aware of the energy that flows between humans and nature. We can actually feel the flow deep within our body as it moves into our innermost being. We honor Earth as a living whole organism, just as we honor human life. She changes with the transitioning seasons, bringing us a new palette of temperature, color, and texture. Earth gives birth to all that we need to live our life in comfort: oxygen, water, food, clothing, security, and soft, comforting beauty. Earth and all living things require our love and appreciation in order to thrive.

We nurture each other as we coexist in peace.

It is nice to add silent words to our in- and out-breath and our steps. Our words will depend on the length of each breath. Some ideas are "love—shared" (between humans and creation), "peace—now," "sharing—now," and so on. Words come easily into our mind as we become more attuned to sharing life with all living things and as we learn to honor all the elements of nature.

As you plan your nature-walking meditation experiences, it is important to notice the elements of nature that bring *you* inner peace and calm. We are unique beings who derive our solace from different environments. Some of us love the ocean and the sandy beach. Some of us love the silence, smell, and feel of a forest of old-growth trees. Some others love the feel of the wide-open spaces and the sight of rolling hills and green fields. Some like the sight and feel of bare rock and rugged mountains with their jutting formations. Others love the flatlands and the feel and sound of wind whipping around them. Some feel at home in a rural mountain village with winding roads and trails for hiking. Those born in cities might feel at home in a large urban area with city parks and walking trails made for quiet moments. The energy of every environment is as unique as people are unique. We obtain the maximum rest and rejuvenation when we can stop, rest, and restore ourselves in an environment that fulfills our deepest inner needs. If we live in an environment that feeds our soul and provides the healing balm that satisfies our deepest emotional needs, we are very lucky indeed. If we don't, we can provide rest and healing for ourselves through our walking meditation and vacationing frequently in the environment that speaks to our heart.

Credit: Taras Chemus

EMOTION WALKING: EMOTIONAL WHOLENESS, ACCEPTANCE, AND RELEASE

The essence of this practice is that when we encounter pain in our life, we breathe into our heart with the recognition that others also feel this. It's a way of acknowledging when we are closing down and of training to open up. When we encounter any pleasure or tenderness in our life, we cherish that and rejoice.

—Pema Chödrön[8]

Walking and breathing meditation work whether we are working on our life issues, are engaged in an emotional-spiritual wholeness journey, or are trying something new that might create a greater sense of well-being. In 1996, when I began walking meditatively, I chose emotional healing as the intent of some of my walks, and I began to monitor my positive thinking. I used positive language as a tool for personal healing. What follows is a

---

[8] Pema Chödrön, *The Pocket Pema Chödrön* (Boulder, CO· Shambhala Publishing, 2008).

more sophisticated way of softening and healing painful emotions.

I feel that some of us will find this walk emotionally and spiritually challenging, Healing is a process, and it is unwise to rush the process by attempting activities that place us in a position to become emotionally exhausted and overwhelmed. Comfort and safety—essentials for emotional growth and emotional health—are the keys to a steady and successful journey toward wholeness. As we learn the directions for the emotion walk, we will use our inner wisdom to decide if this walk is for us at this time. We will continue to match our steps with our breath and combine positive words and phrases to help us to focus in the present moment.

Our life can often take on a hurry-scurry quality that makes us dazed and oblivious, even when we like our jobs and enjoy our friends and family. In times of emptiness and depletion, we often put our emotions aside so we can survive within the overscheduled chaos. There is always more work to complete, some place to go, an appointment to keep, or something that needs to be purchased or fixed. At other times, when we are physically exhausted, our emotions can feel overwhelmingly difficult. We might feel weepy or find it difficult to sleep. A regular daily quiet time and a spiritual practice can help us to regain our equilibrium.

As we practice our meditative breathing and our walking meditation, we gradually reawaken to our own inner wisdom. The walking is a gentle method of accepting ourselves and growing emotionally and spiritually. It allows us enough time and the safety we need to open and embrace our human nature. As we walk in the gentle, unconditional acceptance and love that the universe provides, we create pathways to move from unfeeling and insensitive to sensitive, fully awake, and aware.

Walking to Awaken and Experience Our Emotions

Emotion walking is practiced once we have mastered the art of matching our breaths to our steps during breath walking and nature walking. If we have been breath walking and nature walking for a while, we have already become more comfortable with our emotions, our body, and our lives. We have gained insights, processed information, and are living more productively in the present moment.

The emotion walk allows us to feel our emotions more clearly and encourages us to allow our emotions to flow freely through us. The emotion walk is a process walk. We process our accumulated emotional baggage a little at a time as we practice our breathing and stepping in an atmosphere of acceptance and unconditional love.

In truth, any walking meditation is a catalyst for healing of spirit and emotion. This walk, however, is focused on our whole continuum of emotional experiences, our emotional history and baggage. As we walk, we gradually embrace who we are now and what is real for us now. Because of the walk, we can gradually experience and embrace our whole range of emotions without fear.

All emotions are welcome as we walk. We don't assign good or bad to any emotion. We simply accept emotion as it arises. We allow ourselves to fully experience, without self-criticism, what we need and want in order to achieve emotional balance and heal distress. Our emotions simply are what they are, and we do not judge them. Our reactions to any given emotion create the experience of good or bad. If we accept our reactions without self-judgment, we can accept all our emotions without judgment.

As we walk, we experience a deep, restorative relaxation. Insight arises from our relaxation, and together they ease our painful experiences. The coupling of relaxation with insight and release produces a profound result. Our mind, body, and spirit are working together.

Walking meditation and breathing relaxes and softens our muscles, produces mental clarity, and allows our protective shields to fall away. When the protective shield falls away, we can experience our natural and loving inner nature. The healing balm of pure, unconditional love is emotionally filling, compassionate, and joyous. It creates an atmosphere of forgiveness for ourselves and others. All forgiveness takes place within us first. That change alters our interactions and allows others to respond to us in new and healthier ways.

Healing for One of Us Is Healing for All of Us

All of creation is one energy that takes different animate and inanimate forms. When one of us finds his or her personal, restorative space, the energy of human life and all other forms of life are positively influenced. If all of us could find this internal healing place, conflicts between individuals, communities, and countries would cease. If we all could find this special space, we would care for our Earth home with love and tenderness. Feeling our love and tender care, Earth could heal her deep imbalances. We have wounded her profoundly. We have caused violent, rapid change through our lack of understanding and our unconscious living and by bombing her during war. Yet it is possible to stop all intentional wounding of self, others, and nature.

Simply being aware of our inner core, our inner oasis, is healing. Knowing that we have complete access to it is very reassuring.

Knowing that we have the ability to maintain conscious awareness at each moment of our life creates a keen gratitude. Gratitude creates experiences of deep love of self, and that self-love flows unmodified to all living things.

When we experience a healing emotion walk, we are not walking to heal accumulated emotional pain. *We are healing because we know who we are, and we accept and embrace ourselves and our emotions.* When we walk, we comfort the child within ourselves. The closeness, the flowing motion of the walk, and the acceptance allows our inner child to accept and heal the cause of the wounds. Our clarity and our insight create our healing.

Stopping along the pathway in a nurturing location and gently rocking from side to side while breathing is healing. The nurturing environment softens and soothes us, and the gentle left-to-right rocking is a symbol of safety and love.

When rocking, we use the right and left sides of our body and brain; we employ some of the emotional healing techniques found in many of the energy psychologies. The energy psychologies are gaining in popularity because they are efficient at helping us release troubling thoughts and emotions very quickly, shortening therapy by weeks or even months. (More information about energy psychology is found in chapter 9.)

When we hold our feelings within the soft, gentle embrace of our breath and our walk, the gentle holding softens our resistance as well as the part of us that might be traumatized and hurting. The softness of relaxation allows our emotions to feel fully acknowledged and accepted. The acknowledgment and the acceptance are the healing balm that eases our pain.

We can use emotion walking to heal fear, depression, anger, grief, and any other emotion that is out of balance.

There are no limitations to our emotional healing. When we can allow ourselves to feel what we need to feel without judging ourselves as weak, flawed, or broken, we are on our way to wholeness and happiness.

Acknowledging and Releasing Anger

Many of us have been taught that anger is a negative, disruptive emotion that should be avoided at all costs. Because we were taught to repress our feelings of anger, the feelings frighten us, and the fear causes us deeper emotional pain and distress. When we hold our anger within the soft, accepting embrace created by our emotion walk, we allow ourselves to safely experience our anger. Because we are safe and our emotions are safe in our walking and in our acceptance, our anger does not overcome us. We create no harm to ourselves or others. The acknowledgment of the anger and the safety of the embrace allow the emotion to flow freely through us. The emotional flow, which is both recognition and a release, helps the causes of the anger to begin to heal. During the release, we can employ our left-to-right rocking motion to help increase our level of comfort.

Please know that rocking front to back does not create the result we want. It does not balance or create energetic harmony. Rocking right to left does help us create the balance and harmony we seek.

Acknowledging and Releasing Grief and Loss

When we hold our feelings of grief and loss within a soft, accepting embrace, we allow ourselves to experience the loss that we are grieving. The experience may be quite strong, but we are soothed, and the grief and loss are soothed in the tender embrace of our breath and the rhythm of our walking motion. The acknowledgment of the lost love soothes our aching heart and allows us to heal. Acknowledgment allows us to accept the reality of the loss. Our acceptance of reality helps heal our feelings of separation. The bilateral left-to-right rocking motion helps us release our pain.

When we move from one city to another, we grieve for places and people we have left behind. We grieve for people and pets when they make their transitions into spirit. We grieve for lost or broken artifacts. We grieve for lost opportunities. Because we bring these strong feelings to the gentleness of our emotion walk, we are able to let them go with unconditional love. We sometimes need to stop our walks in a quiet, safe place and allow our emotions to process. We can stop and rock or use other processes described later in this section. We remember that all healing is a process, and it occurs in stages. There will be another emotion walk and another opportunity for healing when we are emotionally and spiritually ready.

Soothing Our Disappointment

Disappointment is an overlooked emotion. It sometimes leads us into a victim state and seems to be the underlying emotional fuel for anger, feelings of grief and loss, and many other potent emotions. It is especially strong in adolescents, young adults, and people who have grown up in dysfunctional, stress-laden families.

This often-forgotten emotion creates deep emotional pain that manifests isolation, detachment, and separation from the ones we love most. Disappointment may be the most disruptive of all emotions. It helps determine whether or not we see the world as a safe place and experience ourselves as worthy.

We can hold the emotion of disappointment in the comfort of our emotion walk. Just as we allow our anger, grief, and loss to become soothed, we can soften and heal the disappointment we feel so deeply within our heart. If we can walk purposefully to create healing for the emotion of disappointment, it often speeds the healing of many other emotions that we consciously recognize.

Handling Strong Emotion

When we walk with a gentle smile that acknowledges the existence of any emotion, the smile on our lips helps us shift our inner perceptions.

This inner shift helps us accept reality. If our emotional pain is too great for us, and our mindfulness practice is not yet developed to the point where we can handle the pain when it arises, there are things we can do during our walk to help ease our emotions. When we greet the pain consciously and mindfully with a welcoming smile, our smile creates feelings of safety, enabling us to process our pain.

Finding Our Way through Intense Emotional Pain

The following directions are straightforward and to the point and are easy to use during times of strong emotion.

1. Stop walking and continue to breathe.

2. Recognize that your naturally deep belly breathing is a powerful means for easing your emotional pain.

3. Continue to breathe, and allow the emotion in your mind and heart to drop down into your belly.

4. Place your hands over your lower abdomen and simply practice deep yet natural and gentle belly breathing. Rocking left to right can be coupled with your breathing.

5. If you are familiar with the Radiant Energies Balance (REB) posture used to create autonomic nervous system balance, use that posture, and practice deep belly breathing. Focus on the emotions that you have dropped into your belly (see directions for this posture in chapter 9).

6. After five to fifteen minutes of breathing in this way, you will feel much better; your body and your heart will feel lighter.

7. Realize that if you continue breathing, walking, and releasing, one day you will be able to fully embrace all of your emotions. The very intense outpourings will cease.[9]

When we feel especially fragile, it is important to spend as much time as possible in an environment that supports the practice of mindfulness. In a mindful environment, we can tend to our seedlings of joy, peace, and compassion. An environment that supports mindfulness is a gentle, loving environment where we are loved, accepted, and safe. In a mindful environment, we have time alone to simply be with ourselves, rest, and heal. In this environment, there is time to process what we need to process. We are consciously held

---

[9] Based on Nguyen Anh-Huong and Thich Nhat Hanh, *Walking Meditation* (Sounds True, Inc., 2006). Adapted with permission of publisher.

in compassion and love. We have no need to be afraid when we have all that we need to work through our pain. Positive health is a journey. We begin where we are now. One step at a time, we heal each aspect of our being, creating wholeness and an overall vigor that vibrates with the joy of today.

Credit: Ivana Cajina

HEALTH WALKING: USING BREATH AND AFFIRMATIONS TO IMPROVE HEALTH

When a heart is at ease, the body is healthy.
—*Chinese proverb*

Health walking helps us accept our health as it is today. Because of that acceptance, we are able to care for our whole selves, as we are in the present moment. It helps us develop a consciousness that provides insight into the origin of our health issues.

The knowledge that flows through us contains information regarding behaviors that support our healing, as well as some of the activities that distract from our healing processes. Our inner core—our place of unconditional love, compassion, and joy—becomes more real to us as we walk. Because our inner core awareness is growing, we are able to be more loving to ourselves and others.

Health walking helps us develop and accept self-responsibility. This acceptance and emotional support eases our concern, giving us the grace to live with our health issues as they are in the moment. It is more than a self-care process. It is a process that allows us to accept what is true. It becomes the vehicle that facilitates recognition and release of the emotions, issues, and perceptions that affect our medical conditions and treatments. The more centered, grounded, and mindful we are and the more connected to our inner joy we are, the easier it is for our body to respond in a positive manner to all healing opportunities.

Our Body Responds to Our Positive Thoughts

We create a gentle smile as we begin our health walk. Our welcoming smile allows us to open to possibility. Because of the walk and our smile, we are able to allow our body, mind, and emotions to soften around our health issues. We become increasingly aware of the miracle of our own lives. In this softening and openness, we find increased energy flow and healing capacity. Our walking practice provides the internal rest and relaxation we need for healing and increases our ability to maintain our mindfulness during our daily activities.

We begin our health walk with "Standing like a Tree." As we ground and center ourselves in preparation for our mindful walk, we relax and become more fully present and now-focused. Our mind is clear, and our focus is increasingly centered on the activity at hand. We listen to our body-mind-emotion-spirit system. Our intuition helps us choose the focus of the walk and leads us to the exact appropriate words needed to move our health forward.

Our Body Believes Every Word We Say

Since words vibrate with a specific energetic frequency, they produce a specific impact. Because of this emotional/ physical impact, our inner language (self-talk) is very important. The more positive and loving our words and thoughts, the greater their positive influence on our overall health. Our body works very hard to give us what we ask for. Our job is to parent ourselves with respect. A good book to read on this subject is Barbara Hoberman Levine's *Your Body Believes Every Word You Say*.

As we focus on the words we will use for our walk, we match the words with our breathing and our stepping, and we begin. We do this so that all aspects of our being are working together to create healing and well-being.

Our words are spoken mentally in unison with each step and each in-breath and out-breath. We might match each word with a step and an in-breath or an out-breath, or we can have two, three, or four words per step and breath. We might opt for phrases like "I choose good health," "I love and accept my body," "I love my sore ankle" (say the name of the afflicted body part), or "I love and care for my pancreas" (say the name of the tissue or organ). In this way, we give our body healing messages over and over for the duration of our walk. We might have one message for a short while and then simply and easily move into another message that seems positive and right for our healing process.

We allow the words and messages to evolve as our mindfulness and clarity deepens. Walking in this way helps us to build upon the health we have today and create an atmosphere that supports our emotional and spiritual growth. We recognize complicating emotions and behaviors that contribute to the overall quality of our health and lives. Better decisions ultimately lead to enhanced self-care and quality of life. A positive adaptation occurs. This is illustrated in a mindfulness chain of thoughts.

Mindfulness Chain

1. Walking meditation
2. Thought stopping
3. Rest and relaxation
4. Deeper connection to life, nature, and the God of our understanding
5. Intellectual, emotional, and spiritual understanding
6. Increased clarity
7. Improved decision-making
8. Better self-care
9. Healing and improved health
10. Higher level of activity and productivity
11. Increased self-esteem
12. Higher degree of satisfaction with life
13. Now-focused living that leads to spiritual awakening

This progression is infinite. Once we reach a particular level of spiritual awakening, we begin the progression all over again. We continue to walk, our rest and relaxation becomes deeper, and we achieve a higher degree of spiritual awakening.

We Are Not the Illness or Our Pain

Our new level of insight might bring powerful emotions to the surface. Unbalanced emotions are always a part of our health issues. We may experience sadness, fear, anger, and many other emotions that complicate our wellness quest. If emotions do arise, we are well equipped to meet them. We welcome the emotions and embrace them, as taught in the emotion walk and mindful breathing. We are multifaceted. We are so much more than the illness or pain we encounter. With acceptance, we are able to allow all of our conflicting emotions to heal. With emotional healing, our body achieves greater balance and ability to function. Our joy of living is deepened.

Each health walk is positive and meaningful and ends with profound gratitude. I always feel happy to be alive and healthy enough to walk, grow, and learn.

The joy of self-understanding is immeasurable.

Part Four

EXPANDING
OUR VISION

Credit: Fernando Gago

Credit: Nicholas Bartos

GOING DEEPER
WITH RADIANT
ENERGIES BALANCE:
A MINDFULNESS-BASED
ENERGY PSYCHOLOGY

*Wisdom, happiness, and courage are not waiting
somewhere out beyond sight at the end of a straight line;
they're part of a continuous cycle that begins right here.
They're not only the ending but the beginning as well.*
—*Benjamin Hoff*[10]

Radiant Energies Balance (REB) is a mindfulness-based energy psychology originated by Phillip Warren, who was a Canadian psychology and music professor. I joined him as a codeveloper in 1999 and have been writing about it, teaching it, and using it in my practice since that time.

REB utilizes what traditional Chinese medicine calls the radiant circuits. The triple warmer and spleen meridians

---

[10] Benjamin Hoff, *The Tao of Pooh* (New York: Dutton, 1982).

work together with the governing and central vessels to create the radiant circuits.

The triple warmer meridian is known as our inner warrior and is responsible for our fight-or-flight response that engages when we sense danger. The spleen meridian is known as our inner mama, providing comfort in times of stress. The governing vessel and the central vessel help fuel our nervous system. The radiant circuits work together to support every organ in our body and to maintain the function of our whole energetic system. When the radiant circuits are engaged, they create feelings of inner harmony and joy.

Because Radiant Energies Balance is an autonomic nervous system balance, it helps regulate blood pressure, heart rate and rhythm, and every other automatic function in our mind-body system. It helps keep us out of fight or flight and helps us reestablish or strengthen our relaxation response. Radiant Energies Balance makes it easier for each of us to recover from trauma, accidents, and any other stressor we might experience. It also assists those of us who have trouble going to and staying asleep. It is tremendously helpful for those who experience fear, anxiety, and phobias.

Instructions for Using the Radiant Energies Balance (REB) Posture

Do not use this technique without the assistance of a professional if you have untreated post-traumatic stress disorder, untreated acute stress disorder, or bipolar disorder. This posture is safe for almost everyone when used as directed. Do not alter the directions.

When the REB posture is engaged, it produces a deep sense of peaceful, meditative relaxation. It is a wonderful adjunct to meditative breathing, especially if we are experiencing high levels of stress, anxiety, or panic.

When intense, troubling emotions arise, they can be very frightening and overwhelming. We are taught to use our mindful breathing skills to allow blocked emotions to flow so we can heal. We can enhance our breathing and healing by engaging the basic REB self-help posture.

Our right hand rests softly under our left breast with our fingers pointing under our left arm. Our left hand rests softly about an inch above our right elbow, hooking our thumb inside the bend of our right arm. If we have the ability to sit, recline, or lean against a solid structure, we can cross our ankles to enhance the REB connection. It does not make any difference which ankle is crossed over the other, and we can change our ankle positions at any time.

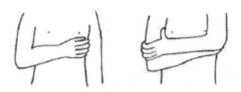

REB Posture

We do not have to try to relax in this posture; the posture relaxes us. Trying to relax more quickly and deeply only postpones the relaxation response. The posture, combined with naturally deep and mindful breathing, automatically produces the relaxation. If we continue to breathe and hold the posture, our body will come into a state of calm. The key is to stay with the posture. The process has the ability to stop the flow of stress hormones from our adrenal glands and balance breathing, heart rate, and possibly blood pressure.

Individuals who are anxious or naturally impatient often are reluctant to stay in the posture long enough to obtain results. People with high anxiety may react with fear to the unfamiliar experience of sudden relaxation. When we relax, especially if we have been stressed for a long time, we experience various body sensations. They are all good! These sensations vary between individuals, and all or none of them may be experienced: feeling heavy all over; a heavy sensation in the chest as tense muscles relax; feeling light and floaty; suddenly hot and sweaty, cold and chilled, or various tingling sensations throughout the body. None of these sensations is uncomfortable but may be surprising if we are not expecting them.

REB and Childbirth

The Radiant Energies Balance posture can be used in many different types of situations, to effect many different types of healing: physical, emotional, spiritual, even generational. I taught Theresa how to use REB to help with her chronic anxiety. She found that it was also useful for coping with the pain of childbirth. She shared:

> *I began therapy with Janet Nestor when I was pregnant with my younger son. I had been suffering from chronic anxiety as well as flashbacks from post-traumatic stress disorder after having been physically attacked. Janet invited me into her comfortable office and ushered me to the sofa. She was warm and nurturing and pleasantly jovial. It*

wasn't long before she suggested that I could benefit from learning and practicing REB. Each time afterwards that I entered her office and sat down, she immediately reminded me of the instructions and asked me to assume the REB posture.

In the beginning, I could not tell any difference, but slowly, as the weeks progressed, I began to notice its effect. My breathing instantly slowed, my thoughts turned slowly inward, and ... shhhhhhh ... within a few moments of sitting down, I could feel a perceptible internal click. My mind and body would shift from the chaotic residual hubbub still clinging to me from my rush to her office through traffic on the interstate, mentally thinking of dozens of things and physically jittery, to the deeply quiet inner knowing that came over me when I began using the REB posture. Janet could even tell from where she sat the moment when something in me shifted, as the adrenaline was receding. I successfully used REB whenever I began to remember my assault and feel the fear and anxiety.

I was so happy to have finally learned something that worked to quell my anxiety.

A few months after meeting Janet, my amniotic water broke. Several hours later, I was in the middle of active labor. My labor and delivery with my older son years before had shown that I was highly allergic to certain types of medications, particularly those used during labor and delivery. I was not allowed to receive an epidural or anesthesia of any kind in order to prevent any correlating complications. The pain, however, was excruciating. My baby was in a position that was causing me to experience back labor. The discomfort did not completely abate between contractions. Each contraction felt like a snug blanket of extreme aching around my low back, with a knife jabbed into my spinal column, radiating pangs of lightning down both of my legs. I felt completely lost and out of control.

At one point, I shifted my position and accidentally brushed one ankle across the other. This feeling instantly reminded me of the sessions I had spent with Janet in her office, practicing the REB posture. I immediately imagined myself back in her office, sitting before Janet, crossing my legs at the ankle. I breathed in a deep inhale and ssssshhhhhhh … there it was, click, the internal shift occurred. Right away, the labor pain became bearable. I felt as if my self, my body, my whole being was part of a universal rhythm and the pain was only a tiny part of that. Instead of feeling attacked and assaulted unjustly by the labor pains, I became a part of the pain, and the sharp edges began to melt. My entire body shifted into a state of deep relaxation. Slowly, the pain radiating down through my legs began to ease, and I no longer felt like a knife was jabbing into my spine. The rough edges became soft.

I kneaded my side and arm with my hands, and my face relaxed. Only a few minutes before, my face had been contorted in pain. The attending nurse noticed the difference. I was checked, and it was discovered that the umbilical cord was dangerously wrapped twice around my baby's neck. The relaxation induced by the REB posture had given me mental alertness and clarity. The nurse instructed me to stop pushing until the certified nurse midwife could untangle the umbilical cord from around my baby's neck. If I could not control what had seemed like involuntary actions of my muscles, my baby could be in danger. The cord could tighten and cut off his flow of oxygen. However, by that point, I was completely relaxed and responsive. The nurse midwife informed me that she had managed to unwind the umbilical cord. She told me that I would then need to control how I pushed my baby out, down at first and then up. I was fully aware and able to follow all of her instructions.

I later remembered the birth of my first son, with two epidurals and numerous medications. During that delivery, I was physically so numb that I could not move or control anything from my waist down, yet I was still in extreme pain, including sciatica in one leg. Mentally, I was dull, confused, panicked, and unresponsive. I could not follow any instructions of the doctor or nurses.

I credit Janet's determination to teach me her REB posture with helping me to deliver a healthy baby boy with no complications. And it has helped me often in times of stress to alleviate any anxiety that has come my way.

Credit: Hymphery Muleba

Ten

BECAUSE WE WALK, WE AWAKEN: GENERATIONAL HEALING

And the end of all exploring will be to arrive where
we started and know the place for the first time.
—*T. S. Eliot* [11]

At some point in our walking and during the contemplation of our walking, we become aware of our identity and our relationship with time. Our concepts change—of past and future, birth and death, beginnings and endings. At some point, a truth will slowly evolve or suddenly spring upon us. All of these things are nothing but human concepts! We use them to define human history or personal history and to communicate about the human experience. When we touch this deeper understanding, we realize that we are simply a part of creation, and creation, in some form, has no end. At this point, we have a different concept of our position in space and our presence in time. We realize that within the universe of creation, we simply

---

[11] T. S. Eliot, *Four Quartets* (San Diego: Harcourt, 1943).

are. We realize that we have permission to *be*, to fully exist and fully experience life. When we experience the fact that we have permission to *be*, we begin to understand the ultimate reality: we *are* a part of creation because we exist. At this point, we instinctively know that all things exist as one.

If we use the analogy of a drop of water in an ocean, we understand. Each individual drop of water is perfectly unique and is a vital part of the ocean. Without each distinct drop, the ocean would not exist. Each of us is a totally unique individual, a part of the sea of human life and a part of the sea of all life as it exists. Human life is not the supreme life-form. All life is important and intelligent and has innate survival instincts. We simply have different skills, roles, and reasons for existence. Without this awareness and deep understanding, it is not possible to fully enjoy being human.

We learn that the body is the shelter for the temple within. Through our daily meditative practice, we learn to access and enter the temple.

Our temple (inner wisdom, center of well-being, soul self) is as large and as roomy as we develop it to be. All of the love, wisdom, contentment, creativity, courage, and power that exists is available to us within our temple. The more time we spend inside, the more we are able to live within the energy that is generated there. Our words and behaviors become kinder, our body heals faster, our mind is clearer and more alert. We function as part of and are at peace with all living things.

Generational Healing

What is time? Is a generation only a measurement of time? Does family history influence the outcome of our lives? Do you and I have the opportunity to create our own life stories—to heal our ties with our ancestors? Does our healing create a new life story for future generations?

Human beings created linear measurement of time in order to bring a sense of continuity into our life and give us a sense of history. This includes the concepts of past, present, and future. Linear time changed existence. It now defines our view of reality.

In a spiritual sense, the only time we have is now, meaning that all life since the creation of Earth is happening now. If we know that all time is now, it is much easier to understand the concept of generational healing. If we believe in a continuum of life (spiritual life, birth, and life in a human body; death as a return to spiritual life), then the following explanation of generational healing takes on a deeper meaning.

When we heal because we are practicing walking meditation, meditative breathing, or another healing technique, we create a line in time that ripples out in all directions. Those in our life today are in the strongest wake and are infinitely affected by our lighter, less-burdened, more spiritually connected and contented footsteps. Those in earlier generations, not living in our households, may be less directly affected, but they too experience the joy of our healing. They find a greater level of peace, joy, and safety themselves because they sense our peacefulness, our acceptance, and our increasingly open emotional state. Those in subsequent generations—our children and their children—experience the waves we make in a similar manner. They are exposed to our positive attitudes, our increased ability to love ourselves and others, and our sense of spiritual connection that is accepting, supportive, and safe.

Each of us has a story that is a description of one's birth, life, and death. Inside, we carry the genetic history of our parents and their parents and earlier generations. We carry the stories of their traumas, successes, adventures, likes and dislikes, life decisions, illnesses, births, and deaths. We carry their guilt, shame, anger, frustration, love, kindness, compassion, and hope.

When we decided to begin our healing journey, we began to heal our life and positively change our stories through self-love, acceptance of reality, and forgiveness. Our love, forgiveness, and acceptance allow current, past, and future generations to break the emotional ties that create so many of the conscious and unconscious attitudes that determine our worldview. Our healing and wholeness relegate the past to the past—where it belongs. Our healing and our love of self allow the future to be lived one day at a time. It gives the youngest generations an opportunity to live in freedom, hope, and love.

What does it look like to live in freedom, hope, and unconditional love? Unconditional love incorporates joy, forgiveness, compassion, inner peace, acceptance, and positive change. With acceptance, we mindfully acknowledge our realities as they exist now.

When Living Within Freedom and Unconditional Love, We Hope to:

- Think positively and act in positive ways
- Honor the natural interdependence of family life
- Allow independence within family togetherness
- Live each day with hopeful, joyous heart
- Develop a positive sense of self, including worthiness
- Experience a sense of belonging
- Make loving, appropriate, reality-based decisions
- Be accountable for our behaviors
- Ask for support when we need and want it
- Embrace peacefulness
- Offer and receive respect
- Feel safe
- Trust
- Enjoy emotional intimacy with family and friends
- Embrace emotional intimacy within our romantic relationship
- Feel compassion for dysfunctional family members (current and past)
- Believe in our personal power and ability to write our own life stories
- Live within our own healthy belief system
- Have fun and laugh a lot
- Live within a healthy life plan, one day at a time
- Love deeply, wisely, and with joy and passion

Activities for Generational Healing

Generational Healing and Walking Meditation—Janet-Style

1. Follow the directions for Walking Meditation—Janet-Style (see chapter 2).
2. Make a list of personal beliefs and perceptions that you want to change.
3. Make a list of the painful emotional ties you would like to forgive and release.

Choose your desired outcome (DO), always remembering to keep words and thoughts positive.

We create our desired outcomes (DO) to meet our specific healing needs. Some suggestions:

Desired Outcome	DO Expressed Positively
Release the shame and guilt I feel	Embrace wholeness, joy, freedom
Release the negativity I feel	Embrace peace, forgiveness, positive thought
Release the disappointment I feel	Embrace acceptance, peace, hopefulness
Release the family history of anxiety	Embrace a positive, peaceful, quiet mind
Release the family history of alcoholism	Embrace clarity, compassion, safety
Release the family history of abuse	Embrace release, well-being, safety
Release feelings of abandonment	Embrace belonging, intimacy, wholeness

As we walk peacefully with our selected DOs, our wise inner nature takes over and helps us understand, heal, and let go of the negativity we have stored within. We find our joy.

As we heal, it is important to keep positive thoughts, joy, and positive outcomes in our minds. It is important to acknowledge and accept our wholeness. We don't have to do anything to become whole; wholeness is a part of us and already exists. Our journeys take us, mindfully and consciously, to what already exists within us.

Generational Healing and Mindful Breathing

Follow the directions for mindful breathing, as presented earlier in the book (see chapter 3).

We breathe and speak a positive word on the in-breath and on the out-breath. We choose companion words that define what we are trying to achieve. We breathe to allow healing to occur. By doing so, we break the ties to dysfunctional and repetitive negative family patterns. Each of the positive words below can be spoken as short phrases in order to extend the breath. Some examples of words and phrases are in the following chart. To enrich our responses, we can utilize the Radiant Energies Balance posture. (Complete instructions are found in chapter 9.)

Generational Healing and Mindful Breathing

Family Issue	In-Breath	Out-Breath
Yelling/Fighting (or reword as a short phrase if you wish to extend the breath)	Peaceful *I am peaceful.*	Content *I am content.*
	Gently *I speak gently.*	Quietly *I respond quietly.*
Dishonesty/ Manipulation	Trust *I can trust.* *I am trustworthy.*	Safety *I am safe.*
	Honest *I am honest.*	Dependable *I am dependable.*
Verbal Abuse	Worthy, Confident	Valued, Safe
Alcoholism/ Addiction	Loving, Peaceful	Accepting, Reality
Sexual Abuse	Safety, Honesty	Honor, Clarity
Abandonment, Neglect	Worthy, Visible	Belong, Wanted
Feeling Invisible	Present, Noticeable	Belong, Wanted
Hostile Divorce	Worthy, Loving	Peaceful, Compassionate
Disappointment, Broken Heart	Hopefulness, Compassion	Trust, Acceptance

Each of us knows what our family wounds are. If we look for family patterns (current and generational), we discover what we want to change and how we want to grow and heal. We allow our higher self to guide us to the specific words and phrases needed to assist the healing of our heart, mind, and emotion.

Acceptance and forgiveness are the essential ingredients that allow generational healing to occur. Most of the time, we believe that acceptance and forgiveness let the guilty person "get by" with bad behavior. Accepting reality and holding ourselves or someone else accountable is part of the process of forgiveness and requires clarity and compassion.

Forgiveness is defined as "letting go" of negative emotions and the associated pain and hurt. When we let go of our pain and hurt, we automatically release the negative energetic tie that exists between ourselves and the person(s) we feel harmed or neglected us. If we are forgiving ourselves, we hold ourselves accountable, make our amends for our wrongdoings, and then we let ourselves off the hook. In the letting go, we find our joy.

Forgiveness sets the forgiver free.

Generational Healing and Radiant Energies Balance

We begin by choosing a desired outcome (DO). We can use the same list we developed for generational healing using Walking Meditation—Janet-Style. For increased relaxation and a deeper outcome, we engage the REB posture during mindful breathing. Doing so allows us to move into our unconscious mind and experience from a witness point of view. Mindful breathing and REB help us balance our autonomic nervous systems and regulate our breathing, blood pressure, and the flow of stress hormones.

If we encounter any emotions or memories that we are not ready to feel or work through, we use the directions given to us in the emotion walk (found in chapter 7). The directions for handling intense emotions help us find our way through them. If we are not ready to heal a specific issue, we simply come back to that issue when we are ready.

Generational Healing and Walking in Wholeness

Walking in wholeness is a beautiful way to build our self-awareness and self-worth. As we do this, our heart expands, and we are able to reach out with compassion and forgiveness to ourselves and our family members, past and present. As we see ourselves as whole, we are less critical and clearer in our understanding. The truth becomes more obvious, and we are able to change our perceptions and beliefs about family members and about our roles in the family dysfunction (we all have a role, regardless of the situation). Our acceptance of truth allows our healing to be real and lasting.

Ours is a healing that reaches across time.

Credit: Christoffer Engstrom

MINDFUL CONSCIOUSNESS

Mindful consciousness is a silent way, a peaceful way
A pathway to joy and peace within.
A pathway that brings me fully present
Nurturing, restorative, and healing.

It is an opportunity to unify and harmonize
my mind, body, spirit, emotions.

An opportunity to celebrate the magnificence
of my birth, my breath, my life
To experience the splendor of myl life
and all life within creation.

An opportunity to experience and celebrate my
oneness with creation. An experience of wholeness.

A healing for all—across time, for all time.

Credit: Aleksandra Sapozhnikova

MORE PATHWAYS TO WHOLENESS: MULTISENSORY, MULTILEVEL LIVING

He wakens me morning by morning, wakens
my ear to listen like one being taught.
—Isaiah 50:4 (RSV)

This section of the book is dedicated to helping us create a stronger sense of wholeness. All methods and forms of mindful breathing and walking meditation are intended to guide us toward a higher spiritual awareness, including self-knowledge, improved self-image, interactions between mind-body-spirit, and a greater understanding of the mutuality of all life-forms.

Some of us have experienced great physical or emotional pain in our lives. We see ourselves as flawed or broken and feel we can never be whole again. Others have not experienced great pain, but we grew up in an unconscious, unfeeling, noncommunicative way, with every second planned. Our parents taught us to believe that quiet time was wasted time. Either way, many of us do not visualize or experience ourselves as whole.

Right now, close your eyes and explore the image you have of yourself. What do you see? The ideal is to have an inner image of your whole body, head to toe, all parts working. The inner image of wholeness is consistent with your emotional-spiritual view of wholeness.

If we see only part of our body when our eyes are closed, we most likely feel broken or injured—mentally, physically, emotionally, or spiritually. As human beings, we have the ability to expand our understanding of wholeness and create a stronger, more expansive perception of ourselves and our energy field. The following exercises are designed to help us with this part of our human journey—the journey to feeling powerful, calm, compassionate, loving, and forgiving—whole.

Walking in Wholeness: Expanding Our Inner Vision

This walk is designed to achieve a slightly different window of understanding. The "Walking in Wholeness" walk is a multisensory experience designed to open insight and intuition. We will experience this walk with our five physical senses of sight, sound, smell, taste, and touch and also our inner senses of inner vision, inner hearing, color, and texture. Nonlocal communication and a multitude of sensory modalities are also involved. We will take a notepad with us so we can begin a "Walking in Wholeness Journal."

Journals are a nice way to remember and honor our psychological-spiritual experiences and keep a record of our growth.

It is not necessary to answer each question below. The questions were created to help us achieve a greater awareness, open our pathways to multilevel sensory experiences, and guide us to our creative and universal soul-self.

Walking in Wholeness Walk

- We begin this walk in the same way we begin most of our walking meditations. We take a minute or two to simply stand in *wu-chi* and experience groundedness and our presence of being.

- In this walk, we are not concentrating on matching our steps with our breath. We are focusing on our multisensory image of wholeness. We are learning who we are and experiencing ourselves as fully human at all levels of our being.

- As we begin our first steps, using an inner vision, we imagine that we are seeing ourselves walk. We visualize, head to toe, the front of our body in walking motion. We notice our posture. Is our posture straight, bent, or rigid? Are our eyes softly focused and looking forward and to the ground? We notice our face and our expression. Are we gently smiling? Are we frowning? Do we appear angry? How are our arms and hands moving with each step? Are our arms and hands in tune with our steps? We notice our legs and feet as they move through each step. We notice our gait. Is it smooth and even? Do we appear relaxed and comfortable in our walking motion? How would strangers perceive us if they saw us walking toward them? Do we appear peaceful? Would we be perceived as approachable? When we feel fully aware of ourselves from this perspective, we move to the next visualization.

- We begin to see ourselves from the side. How do we appear as we visualize ourselves in this manner? How do we visualize our arms and legs as we move through each step? How do our hips and legs move through each step? We notice our posture. Is our spine erect? Is our head bowed down in thought? Do we appear sad? Do our body movements signify something is wrong? Is our body moving with a bounce? Do we appear happy and approachable? Do our movements seem labored? How would someone viewing us from the side perceive us?

- Now we begin to visualize ourselves walking from the back. How would we look walking behind ourselves? Are our shoulders high and tight, or are they soft and relaxed? How do our hips move with each step? Are they moving fluidly, or is the motion stiff or awkward? How about the swing of our arms as they move with our steps? Is the movement stiff and tight, or are our arms moving smoothly in a natural, relaxed way? Would the person behind us perceive an emotion? What image do we portray to a stranger walking behind us?

Gaining Multisensory Wisdom, Self-Awareness, and Intuition

We now shift to a deeper, multisensory focus. We will use our physical senses of sight, smell, sound, touch, and taste, as well as more subtle senses that are not as familiar to some of us. We will explore intuition and insight at a fully conscious level. We hope to tap into the universal energy flow that contains the universal consciousness of our Creator.

- **Touch:** How do our feet feel as they touch the earth with each step? How does the earth feel under our feet? Is the ground smooth or rocky? Are our steps comfortable? How does our body feel as it is touched by a breeze or by the atmosphere and temperature of the day? How do we feel as the temperature and atmosphere touch our skin, our clothing, our hair? How does our breath feel as it touches our nose or our lips as we breathe in and out? If we are walking with someone, we reach out and take his or her hand. What does it feel like to have another person's hand holding our hand? How does the temperature of the person's skin feel against our skin? What is the texture of his or her skin? What do we sense in his or her touch? What information can we obtain through the person's touch? Can we sense his or her emotion? Can we sense his or her mood?

- **Smell:** As we walk, what do we smell? Is there a scent floating on the breeze? Are flowers blooming? Is there a factory nearby? Do we smell newly mowed grass? Do we smell damp earth? Are there animals around that might have a scent? If there is water, do we smell the water, the fish? If it is raining or snowing, do we smell the rain or the snow? Do we notice the scent of the sunlight as different from the scent of a shaded area? What about our body as we walk? How do we interpret the scent of our own body? Is the scent pleasant? What does it mean if the smell is not pleasant? If we are walking with others, do we notice their scent? What information can we gain from our ability to smell? Can we smell emotion? Can we smell various moods? Can we smell danger? Can we smell excitement? Can we smell health and wellness in ourselves, in others, and in Earth herself?

- **Sound:** What do we hear as we walk? Do we hear birds singing in the distance? Do we hear traffic nearby? Do we hear a plane flying overhead? Do we hear the sound of our feet touching the earth as we walk? Do we hear the sounds of flowing water? Do we hear a frog jump into the water? Do we hear any animals nearby, maybe a squirrel in a tree or something moving through the underbrush along our path? What if all we hear in the environment is silence? How do we interpret what we hear? How do we feel about what we hear? Does it make us happy, sad, or introspective? Do we hear children playing in the distance or people talking somewhere nearby? If we do hear voices, what information does that bring to us? Can we hear our heartbeats? Do we hear our breath as we breathe? Do we hear anyone else breathing? Do we hear the trees? Does the earth have a sound?

- **Taste:** Do we taste the breeze as it flows around us? Is there a scent in the air so tangible that we taste it? Does the taste of a meal, a cup of coffee, or toothpaste distract us? We often swallow as we walk. What does it taste like to swallow? If it is raining or snowing, do the drops of water or flakes of snow have a taste? If it is hot and humid, does the humidity have a taste? Is there a taste that is exclusive to walking? What does the nectar of a blossom taste like to a butterfly? If we happen upon something frightening or hysterically funny, do these emotions have a taste? In general, do emotions have a taste?

- **Vision:** What do we see as we walk? Does what we see change our perceptions of the walk? How do our feet look as they touch the earth in a step? Do we have an emotional response to the sight of our feet stepping forward? What are the details of our walking paths, and what do we glean from those details? What does the sky look like? If it is raining or snowing, how do the droplets look in the air as they pass by? Do we see anything flying about—a bird, a fly, a butterfly, a dragonfly? Can we see the air itself? If it is foggy, what does the fog look like? If we are walking in the morning dew, how does the dew appear to us? If we are hot and sweaty, what does our skin look like, covered with our own moisture? Does the sight of something pleasant change our mood or increase our depth of feeling? Do our visual experiences affect our physical experiences, our emotional experiences, or our spiritual experiences? If we close our eyes, can we see the path and our surroundings with our inner eyes?

- **Our more esoteric senses:** What do we *sense* about our environment? Is it safe? Are we getting any feelings about the area where we are walking? What is the history of the path and the area? Who has walked here before us? Is it a happy place? Does the area feel heavy, sad, or neglected? Do we feel any emotion coming from anything in the environment? If there are trees nearby, we stand by one and reach out and touch it. Do we sense the life within the tree? Are there any messages coming from the tree? Can we hear it speak? Can we feel its energy? If we are in a rocky area, we can reach out and touch a rock formation or pick up a stone from the ground. What is the experience of touching the rock? What do we sense about the rock formation or the stone? What is its history? Is there life within the rock? Does the rock have any energy?

If we are near water, we can stand along the edge of the river, stream, lake, or puddle. What do we sense as we look at the water? Is the water deep? Is the water clean? Can we communicate with the water? What story is the water telling us? What life-forms live in the water we are examining? We can notice the differences between standing in the sunlight and standing under trees. What does the energy of sunlight feel like? What does the energy of a shaded area feel like? We notice the feeling of standing by flowers. How do the flowers feel? Is there any communication? Do they have a presence? Do they evoke any emotion?

How does it feel to walk by a building or a house? What does the building or house share with us as we walk by or stand near it? Are there people inside the structure? Does the structure evoke any emotion? Can we sense the history of the structure by standing near it?

What do we sense about ourselves as we walk? How is our body doing? Is our body giving us any messages, and if so, what are they? Do we perceive any feelings about our health or a situation in our lives? Do we notice any particular area of our body? If we do feel a specific area of our body, what does that mean? Is there an inner voice speaking about our health?

We notice the difference between walking beside someone and walking alone. Is there a difference in our comfort or in our feelings of safety? If we're walking with others, we notice the quality of their movements. What does the quality of their movements communicate to us? Can we sense any emotion as we walk beside another person?

If there are animals nearby, we stop and watch them. What do we intuit (learn) about the animals? Are they communicating with us in any way? Do they fear us? If the animals are in a group, are they communicating with each other? Can we feel or sense their comfort level as they interact in their group? Do they sense our level of comfort with them?

As our walk ends, we take a moment to jot down our experiences so we can remember them. Writing down our experiences gives us the ability to collect information and deepen our conscious understanding. If we are walking in a group, it might be nice to discuss our experiences together.

Wholeness: A Bioenergetic Self-Guided Meditation

I created this exercise for my personal healing journey, and I share various versions of it with my clients on a regular basis. The exercise can be practiced daily. If we have physical health issues or any sort of difficult emotional history or trauma, I suggest practicing the exercise as often as possible. It is deeply soothing and healing and meant to help us contact our authentic self—the one part of us that is exquisitely formed, whole, unified, and at perfect peace.

- We place our hands on our back at our kidney area. Palms face our back if we can hold them there in comfort. If not, we use the back of our hands. We move our hands in a circular fashion, starting in the center of our back and moving toward the outside of our body. We massage our kidneys in this bilateral (both sides), circular way for a minute or two.

- Standing quietly, feet shoulder-width apart, knees slightly bent, we begin to draw the infinity symbol (figure eight) with our abdomen and hips.

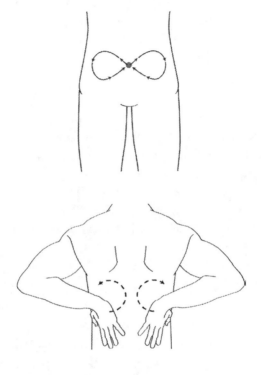

We keep our hips facing forward and imagine that our belly button is the point of a pencil. We use the "pencil" (belly button) to draw the infinity symbol, and we keep our concentration on our abdominal area as we move. Gradually, we learn to allow our body to automatically bring us back to center. We do this movement for a minute or two. The balancing effects are cumulative.

- Standing quietly with our infinity symbols completed, hands resting at our kidney area, we begin the visualization. We breathe quietly from our abdomen, and let our shoulders soften and drop. We visualize a white or yellow light filling our entire body from head to toe. We take as long as necessary to see the light fill us completely. It is very important to see our whole self filled with light.

- Once we see our whole self filled with white or yellow light, we go deeper into the meditation and begin to visualize our nervous system, especially our head, neck, and spine. Our nervous system appears to us as iridescent blue.

- Once we have our nervous system in view, we leave that mental picture and begin to visualize a translucent, very pale pink light, filling our entire body. It is very important to see our whole self filled with this light, from our crown to the tips of our toes. This light is extremely soothing and healing. We stay within this light until we feel we have completed the exercise. If we have any physical or emotional pain or an illness, we stay in this light as long as we feel comfortable doing so.

When we feel ready, we simply open our eyes and come back into our quiet, conscious mind, feeling wonderfully relaxed and soothed. If we are preparing to sleep, we climb into bed and drift into a sound slumber.

Credit: Nathan Dumlao

BELIEF

Silence.

We are born from silence.
If we live from the silence within, we know our
wholeness lives there too. It is limitless, eternal,
trustworthy, joyous, compassionate, loving, and real.
Wholeness is not broken. It cannot be
broken, as each piece is part of the whole
and contains the mystery of the whole.

We cannot run from wholeness or turn away from
it. It goes with us because we are wholeness.
I look at my finger and it is not only a finger. It
is part of a hand that is part of an arm, that is
part of a shoulder, that is part of a body, which is
part of creation, and creation is wholeness.

This truth is challenging to understand. We
cannot find wholeness because it is not lost.

We are wholeness. When our mind is quiet and
still, our heart is open, and our trust is strong. Trust
turns and looks straight into our eyes and speaks:
"Here I am, I am wholeness. I have always been
here. I was with you before you were born, and I
remain throughout time, because I am with you."

It is up to us to live our life in wholeness, to turn
to it and grasp it through conscious living.

Wholeness is the part of us that we touch from time
to time when we pray, meditate, and contemplate.

The more we touch our wholeness, the more
we believe in its existence. It is our belief in the
existence of our wholeness that makes us whole.

Part Five

ET CETERA

Credit: Hans Ripa

Credit: Deva Darshan

ADDENDUM

LIST OF VIRTUES

Virtues are positive aspects of the self. They define love, live in your heart, and help create the vocabulary that produces your thoughts and verbal interactions.

As you bring these positive energies more fully into your heart, you begin to notice that you are happier and mentally and emotionally healthier.

All the virtues can be used as focal points for mindful breathing and walking meditation. For example, you could speak "listening" on the in-breath and "understanding" on the out-breath, or "I am listening" on the in-breath and "I understand" on the out-breath. Experiment with spoken virtues that lift you up and empower you.

There are many, many heart virtues and not all of them are listed below. You can create a list of your own. As you make your list and embrace the individual virtues, you will expand your awareness and your understanding of your life and why you are alive at this time in history.

Quietly, softly, fill your pathways with many virtuous steps and pleasant, joyful thoughts.

Acceptance
Accountability
Adaptability
Alertness
Balance
Beauty
Belief
Centeredness
Choice
Clarity
Comfort
Communication
Compassion
Compromise
Consciousness
Consistency
Contentment
Courteousness
Creativity
Dependability
Devotion
Diversity
Earnestness
Education
Empathy
Excitement
Expressiveness
Exuberance
Faith
Faithfulness
Fitness
Flow
Focus
Forgiveness
Friendliness
Friendship
Generosity

Gentleness
Goodness
Gratitude
Harmony
Healing
Health
Honesty
Honor
Hopefulness
Humility
Humor
Insight
Joy
Kindness
Laughter
Lightheartedness
Listening
Love
Loyalty
Mercy
Naturalness
Noticing
Nurturing
Obedience
Openness
Opportunity
Passion
Patience
Peacefulness
Perceptiveness
Poise
Positivity
Power
Prayer
Presence
Purity
Radiance

Reconciliation
Reflection
Relaxation
Responsiveness
Rest
Reverence
Rootedness
Safety
Satisfaction
Silence
Simplicity
Sincerity
Smile
Softness
Stillness
Straightforwardness
Strength
Supportiveness
Sureness
Tactfulness
Teaching
Tenacity
Tenderness
Thoughtfulness
Transformation
Truthfulness
Understanding
Unification
Vibrancy
Vigilance
Vigor
Vision
Vitality
Wakefulness
Warmth
Wholeness
Wisdom

DEFINITIONS

Mindfulness: A Loving Return to Self-Awareness

Mindfulness refers to now-centered living. We are observant but never judgmental of ourselves or others. We think before taking action, practice self-awareness, and are connected to self and to life.

Mindful Breathing

Mindful breathing is conscious breathing and refers to the awareness of our in- and out-breaths, including the length and depth of each breath. Slower breathing facilitates greater levels of relaxation.

Walking Meditation

Thich Nhat Hanh is considered the modern-day father of this ancient mindfulness practice. It is a moving meditation that includes conscious breathing and slow, purposeful steps that teach practitioners to honor themselves, nature, and Earth. Like resting meditation, it facilitates mind-body-spirit transformation, focus, clarity, and a sense of inner peacefulness.

Emotional Mindfulness: Emotional Awareness

Mindful breathing and walking meditation create emotional flow, as opposed to emotional stagnation. It includes an awareness of how each emotion creates a unique sensory response that positively or negatively impacts our overall sense of health, wholeness, and overall well-being.

Mindfulness Lifestyle

A mindfulness lifestyle refers to a life lived in awareness of a conscious connection to self, life, others, nature, and creation. It involves honoring nature and living in balance with nature, friends, family, our community, and society as a whole.

Energy Psychology: Meridian-Based and Chakra-Based Energy Information Therapy

Many types of energy psychology work with the same meridians that acupuncture uses to release imbalanced or stagnant energy. Some use the chakra system to create energetic balance and healing. Energy psychology addresses post-traumatic stress disorder, anxiety, panic, depression, chronic pain, and most human conditions. These therapies are considered to be brief therapies, meaning they shorten the time a person is in therapy.

Some Common Energy Psychology Modalities

- **EFT**: Emotional Freedom Technique—Gary Craig
- **REB**: Radiant Energies Balance—Phillip Warren and Janet Gallagher Nestor
- **TFT**: Thought Field Therapy—Roger Callahan
- **TAT**: Tapas Acupressure Technique—Tapas Fleming
- **BSFF**: Be Set Free Fast—Larry Nims
- **EDxTM**: Energy Diagnostic and Treatment Methods—Fred Gallo

Virtues: The Various Characteristics of Love

Virtues are positive, heartfelt feelings and beliefs that we choose, accentuate, and develop for the purpose of living more fully and positively. Modern psychology might call them positive character traits or attributes.

REFERENCES

Chödrön, Pema. *The Pocket Pema Chödrön* (Boulder, CO: Shambhala Publishing, 2008).

Eliot, T. S. *Four Quartets* (San Diego: Harcourt, 1943).

Hoberman Levine, Barbara. *Your Body Believes Every Word You Say* (Fairfield, CT: Words Work Press, 2000).

Hoff, Benjamin. *The Tao of Pooh* (New York: Dutton, 1982).

Lao Tzu. *Complete Works of Lao Tzu*. Translated by Hua-Ching Ni (Santa Monica: Seven Star Publications Group, 1979).

Nestor, James. *Breath: The New Science of a Lost Art* (London: Penguin Life, 2020).

Nguyen, Anh-Huong and Thich Nhat Hanh. *Walking Meditation* (Boulder, CO: Sounds True, Inc., 2006).

Sherman, James R. *Rejection: How to Survive Rejection and Promote Acceptance* (Golden Valley, MN: Pathway Books, 1982).

Spalding, Baird T. *Life and Teaching of the Masters of the Far East*, Vol. 1 (Marina del Rey, CA: DeVorss & Company, 1924)

RECOMMENDED BOOKS

Carpenter, Krista. *The Empath's Workbook: Practical Strategies for Nurturing Your Unique Gifts and Living an Empowered Life* (Emeryville, CA: Rockridge Press, 2020).

Eden, Donna. *Energy Medicine: Balancing Your Body's Energies for Optimal Health Joy and Vitality* (New York: Penguin, 2008).

Eger, Edith. *The Gift: 12 Lessons to Save Your Life* (New York: Scribner, 2020).

Houston, Jean. *A Mythic Life—Learning to Live Our Greater Story* (New York: Harper One, 1996).

McTaggart, Lynne. *The Power of Eight: Harnessing the Miraculous Energies of a Small Group to Heal Others, Your Life, and the World* (New York: Atria Books, 2017).

Merk, Cornelia, and Janet G. Nestor. *Revolutionize Your Health: How to Take Back Your Body's Power to Heal* (Bloomington, IL: AuthorHouse, 2018).

Ni, Maoshing. *Secrets of Self-Healing: Harness Nature's Power to Heal Common Ailments, Boost Your Vitality, and Achieve Optimum Wellness* (New York: Penguin, 2008).

Ober, Clinton, and Stephen T. Sinatra, et al. *Earthing: The Most Important Health Discovery Ever!* (Laguna Beach: Basic Health Publications, Inc., 2010).

Williams, Mark, and John Teasdale, et al. *The Mindful Way through Depression: Freeing Yourself from Chronic Unhappiness* (New York: Guilford Press, 2007).

Credit: Dave Hoefler

PERFECT HARMONY

The peace of this place
The life in this place
Brings me inward to a perfect harmony
With the spark that was placed within me
That is meant to burst into a passionate flame.
The peace of this place
The life in this place
Stills my heart to a pure silence
Where I become the love that
I was meant to become.

Follow Janet G. Nestor on Social Media

Website
www.mindfulpathways.com

Twitter
Pathways to Wholeness @JanetNestor

Facebook
https://www.facebook.com/PathwaystoWholeness/

LinkedIn
https://www.linkedin.com/in/janetgnestorlcmhc